Job Title Index to SIC Codes

Job Title Index
to SIC (Standard Industrial
Classification) Codes

by
Richard S. Lea

McFarland & Company, Inc., Publishers
Jefferson, North Carolina, and London

Library of Congress Cataloging-in-Publication Data

Lea, Richard S.
  Job title index to SIC (Standard industrial classification) codes.

  Bibliography: p. 91.
  1. United States — Occupations — Classification —
Indexes. 2. United States. Office of Management
and Budget. Statistical Policy Division. Standard
industrial classification manual — Indexes. I. Title.
HB2595.L43 1988   331.7'0012   87-43167

ISBN 0-89950-311-X (acid-free naturai paper)

Printed in the United States of America.

McFarland & Company, Inc., Publishers
  Box 611, Jefferson, North Carolina 28640

This book is dedicated
to frustrated job seekers everywhere.
Hang in there!

Contents

Contents

8

Contents

Introduction

At the San Diego Public Library, where I work in the Directory Services department, people come in every day asking for help in finding a job. Often they have been referred to our section by an employment agency or job counselor in order to use our business and trade directories. These directories aren't set up just for job seekers; they are primarily marketing and buying tools. They aren't arranged by type of work, but by product or service, classified by SIC (Standard Industrial Classification) code. This arrangement confuses many job hunters, who often go away frustrated and discouraged. *Job Title Index to SIC Codes* is an attempt to demystify the SIC code system and turn it to the job seeker's advantage in trying to find suitable employment.

The SIC code system is based on the federal government's *Standard Industrial Classification Manual* (prepared by the Office of Management and Budget). This manual is commonly referred to as the SIC (pronounced "sick") code manual and is the standard index to company classifications nationwide. Most business and trade directories use this system of company classification in at least one of its possible four-digit levels. *Job Title Index* links job titles to appropriate companies by means of SIC codes at the three-digit level (selected as preferable to the four-digit level because of the three-digit's broader applications). The job titles are mostly from the current *Occupational Outlook Handbook* (a Department of Labor publication), and the SIC code numbers are taken from the 1987 *Standard Industrial Classification Manual*.

There is no getting around a thorough preparation before you actually start sending your resumes to companies. First you need to know what kind of work you want to do. If you don't know, check the *Dictionary of Occupational Titles*, the *Occupational Outlook Handbook*, or other employment reference sources to pin down your occupational choices. Then you need to know what companies or government agencies employ people that do your kind of work. That's where *Job Title Index* comes in: It translates your job title into an SIC code, which you can then use in conjunction with a business or trade directory to compile a list of companies that hire people in your chosen job field. This method can be effectively used anywhere in the United States where Standard Industrial Classification codes are used—which is almost everywhere.

11

Introduction

This book does not pretend to cover all possible job titles or all possible SIC codes to fit each job title. The choice of which SIC code(s) to list for each job title proved difficult. In compiling this book, I based my choices on the "Places of Employment" sections of the *Occupational Outlook Handbook*, newspaper "help wanted" ads, civil service job announcements, the *Dictionary of Occupational Titles*, the SIC code manual itself, and common sense.

Job Title Index to SIC Codes cannot give you company names all by itself. It needs to be used with one or more business directories having a SIC code classification of companies (see the *Bibliography* beginning on page 91 of this book). And certainly *Job Title Index* cannot replace other, more general career guidance works, which can help you plan your job search thoughtfully and effectively. What *Job Title Index* provides that other career reference sources do not is SIC codes to match job titles, for all job seekers of all types and ages. From cradle maker (SIC code 251) to grave digger (SIC code 179), you will find here a government SIC code to match up with almost any job title. You can then match those SIC codes to company names listed in business and trade directories to start that well-balanced job-hunting list.

How to Use This Book

1. Look first in the *Job Titles* section of this book (page 15) for the particular job title(s) you are interested in.

2. Copy down the paragraph number listed after these job title(s). (It will be a three-part number, consisting of a number in bold, a capital letter, and another number, such as "13A1."

3. Turn to the *Occupations Outline* section of this book and locate the paragraph number that you copied down.

4. Read that paragraph and copy down any SIC code numbers (e.g. 33, 334) listed in that paragraph.

5. Locate a business or trade directory that classifies companies by SIC codes and encompasses the geographic area you would like to work in. (Several directories are listed in the *Bibliography*.)

6. Look up in the directory the SIC code(s) you copied down from the *Occupations Outline* section of this book.

7. There you should find a list of company names representing companies that have been known to hire people in the job classification(s) you are interested in.

8. If you just want to browse around the job spectrum:

   a. Look through the Table of Contents and follow up whatever interests you.

   b. Skim through *Job Titles* at random.

   c. Look through the *SIC Code List* section of this book and see how these classifications are organized.

   d. Look through a local business directory. Look up some of these SIC codes your browsing uncovered and see what kinds of companies turn up.

Note: Occasionally you may come up with a SIC code that has no companies listed after it in the local business directory you are using. This sometimes happens when that type of company is found only in certain geographic or climatic regions (for example, you wouldn't find Ski Resorts in the San Diego Chamber of Commerce Directory because it doesn't snow in San Diego). Also, certain types of manufacturing are done only in certain states, so you won't find companies with those SIC codes in other states.

Job Titles

Abbreviations:

MM   *merchant marine*
occ.   *occupational*
occs.   *occupations*
ops.   *operators*
wkrs.   *workers*

Able seamen **7B2**
Abstractors **2E22**
Academic specialists **4B1**
Account clerks **2A1**
Account clerks, new, in banking **2C1**
Account collectors **2A3**
Account executives **5A11**
Account managers **2E1**
Accountants **2E1**
Acoustical carpenters **6B24**
Acquisitions librarians **4B1**
Actors, actresses **13A1**
Actuarial clerks **2A11**
Actuaries **2D1**
Adding and calculating machine operators **2A6**
Adjusters, claim **2D2**
Adjustment clerks **2E19**
Administrative:
   analysts **2E5**
   and related occs. **2E**
   assistants **2E5**
   dieticians **10F1**
   secretaries **2A9**
Administrators:
   health services **10F3**
   medical records **10F4**
   mining **16A6**

   public **2E17**
   salary and wage **2E12**
Admissions counselors **2E6**
Advertising:
   agency personnel **2E2**
   consultants **2E2**
   copy writers **2E2**
   executives **2E2**
   personnel **2E2**
   workers **2E2**
Advisors, foreign student **2E6**
Aerial advertising personnel **2E2**
Aerobic dance instructors **14B18**
Aeronautical technicians **8G3**
Aerospace engineers **8B1**
Agents:
   agricultural extension **12C1**
   extension **12C1**
   F.B.I. **3E3**
   insurance **5A5**
   manufacturers' **5A6/5A14**
   passenger **7A5**
   purchasing **2E14**
   real estate **5A8**
   reservation **7A5**
   special **3E2**
   station **7C9**
   travel **5A13**
Agribusiness occs. **15C**

Agricultural:
    accountants **15C1**
    commodity graders **3E10**
    communicators **15C4**
    economists **15C3**
    engineers **8B2**
    extension agents **12C1**
    journalists **15C4**
    marketing specialists **15C2**
    pilots **15B8**
    quarantine inspectors **3E10**
    school teachers **15C5**
    service occs. **15B**
    technicians **8G3**
Agriculture occs. **15**
Agronomists **8D2**
Aides:
    casework **12C3**
    employment **12C3**
    geriatric **10D3**
    homemaker-home health
        10D3
    library **4B2**
    nursing **10D3**
    occupational therapy **10E2**
    physical therapy **10E4**
    psychiatric **10D3**
    social service **12C3**
    teacher **4A7**
Air-conditioning and refrigeration
  mechanics **9B1**
Air-conditioning, heating and
  refrigeration technicians **8G3**
Air-conditioning mechanics **9B1**
Air safety inspectors **3E10**
Air traffic controllers **7A1**
Airplane:
    mechanics **7A2**
    pilots **7A3**
Alarm (burglar) installers and
  repairers **3F5**
Alcohol inspectors **3E10**

All-round machinist **1B1**
Amateur sports coaches **14B8**
Ambulance attendants **10C3**
Amusement concessions and rides
  ops. and wkrs. **14B2**
Amusement occupations **14B**
Amusement park ops. and
  wkrs. **14B1**
Analysts:
    administrative **2E5**
    job **2E12**
    systems **2B3**
Animal breeders **15B2**
Animal caretakers
  (nonfarm) **15B11**
Animal farming **15A4**
Animal show ops. and
  wkrs. **14B3**
Announcers:
    radio **13C3**
    television **13C3**
Anthropologists:
    applied **11A1**
    linguistic **11A1**
    medical **11A1**
    physical **11A1**
    urban **11A1**
Anthropometrists **11A1**
Appliance repairers **9B2**
Appraisers, real estate **5A8**
Arcade ops. and wkrs. **14B4**
Archeologists **11A1**
Architects **13B1**
    landscape **13B7**
Archivists **11A4**
Arena (sports) ops., promoters
  and wkrs **14A1**
Arrangers, music **13A3**
Art school teachers **4A6**
Artificial breeding:
    distributors **15B3**
    technicians **15 B3**

Artificial inseminators **15B3**
Artists **13B2**
    graphic **13B2**
    performing **13A**
Artists' models **5A7**
Arts, performing occs. **13**
Assemblers **1D1**
    in photographic laboratories
      1D14
Assessors, real and personal
  property — for tax
  purposes **2E3**
Assignment clerks **2A11**
Assistant traffic engineers **8B13**
Assistants:
    administrative **2E5**
    casework **12C3**
    hotel **2E9/3A2**
    instrument **8G5**
    library **4B2**
    management **2E5**
    medical laboratory **10C4**
    medical occs. **10C**
    nursing **10D3**
    occupational therapy **10E2**
    optometric **10C7**
    physical therapy **10E4**
    printing press **1C5**
Astrogeologists **8C1**
Astronomers **8F1**
Astrophysicists **8F1**
Athletic club (membership) ops.
  and wkrs. **14B12**
Attendants:
    ambulance **10C3**
    dining car **7C5**
    dining room **3B3**
    flights **7A4**
    gasoline service station **5A4**
    hospital **10D3**
    lobby **14B20**
    mess **7B2**

    nursing **10D3**
    parking **7D5**
    personal **3D1**
Attorneys **2E8**
Audio control technicians **8G1**
Audiologists **10E5**
Audiovisual specialists **4A8**
Auto-glass mechanics **9B4**
Automatic mounters **1D14**
Automatic print developers **1D14**
Automation specialists,
  library **4B1**
Automobile:
    air-conditioning specialists
      9B4
    body repairers **9B3**
    mechanics **9B4**
    painters **1D2**
    parts counter wkrs. **5A1**
    radiator mechanics **9B4**
    sales wkrs. **5A2**
    service advisors **5A3**
    transmission specialists **9B4**
Auxiliary nursing wkrs. **10D3**

Babysitters **3D1**
Baggage porters **3C5**
Bakers **3B2**
    manufacturing **1D20**
Band (mil.) directors **13A3**
Bank:
    clerks **2C1**
    managers **2C2**
    mortgage processing clerks
      2A13
    officers **2C2**
    bank tellers **2C3**
Banking occs. **2C**

Baptist ministers **12B1**
Barbers **3C1**
Barmaids **3B1**
Bartender helpers **3B1**
Bartenders **3B1**; train **7C1**
Baseball (little league) coaches
    14B8
Baseball players, managers and
    owners (professional) **14A1**
Basketball players, coaches and
    owners (professional) **14A1**
Batboys, professional **14A1**
Beauticians **3C3**
Beauty:
    consultant models **5A7**
    operators **3C3**
Bell captains **3C2**
Bellhops **3C2**
Bench:
    carpenters **6B26**
    coremakers **1A3**
    molders **1A2**
    technicians, ophthalmic **1A13**
Bibliographers **4B1**
Bill collectors **2A3**
Billboard advertising personnel
    2E2
Billiard hall ops. and wkrs. **14B5**
Billing machine operators **2A6**
Bindery wkrs. **1C6**
Biochemists **8D1**
Biographers **11A4**
Biological oceanographers
    8C4/8D2
Biological technicians **8G3**
Biologists **8D2**
Biomedical:
    engineers **8B3**
    equipment repairers **9B25**
Blacksmiths **1D3/7C7**
Blasters **6B23**
Blue-collar worker supervisor **1D4**

Boat-engine mechanics **9B5**
Boatswain **1D4/7B2**
Body repairers, automobile **9B3**
Boiler tenders **1D6**
Boilermaker occs. **1D5/7C7**
Book publishers **13C7**
Book store ops. and wkrs.,
    retail **5A9a**
    (new) **5A9ai**
    (used) **5A9aii**
Bookbinders **1C6**
Bookkeeper, general **2A1**
Bookkeeping:
    machine ops. **2A6/2C1**
    workers **2A1**
Botanists **8D2**
Bowling alley ops. and wkrs.
    14B6
Bowling-pin-machine mechanics
    9B6
Box office cashiers **2A2**
Brake mechanics, automobile **9B4**
Brake operators, train **7C2**
Branch managers, bank **2C2**
Breeders, animal **15B2**
Breeding:
    distributors, artificial **15B3**
    technicians, artificial **15B3**
Bricklayers **6B1**
Broadcast technicians **8G1**
Brokerage clerks **5A11**
Brokers:
    commodity **15C2**
    customers', securities
        business **5A11**
    insurance **5A5**
    real estate **5A8**
    stock **5A11**
Buckers, logging **8A2**
Builders, operative **6B5**
Building:
    custodians **3A1**

inspectors **3E9**
managers **2E20**
Burglar alarm installers and
　repairers **3F4**
Burner (gas) mechanics **9B1**
Burner (oil) mechanics **9B1**
Bus mechanics **9B20**
Bus parts counter workers **5A1**
Bus drivers (intercity) **7D1**
Bus drivers (local transit) **7D2**
Business machine repairers **9B7**
Business school teachers **4A6**
Butlers **3D1**
Buyers **2E4**
Buyers (foreign) **2E4**

Cabinetmakers **6B26**
Cable splicers, telephone **9A3**
Calculating machine ops. **2A6**
Cannery workers **1D21**
Captains, bell **3C2**
Captains (MM) **7B1**
Car checkers **2A11**
Car repairers, train **7C7**
Card-tape-converter ops. **2B1**
Career planning
　counselors **2E6/12A4**
Caretakers:
　　animal – nonfarm **15B11**
　　poultry **15B6**
　　private household **3D1**
Carpenters: **6B2**
　　bench **6B26**
　　ship (MM) **7B2**
Carriers, mail **3F1**
Cartographers **11A3**
Cartographic technicians **8G3**
Casework aides **12C3**
Cashiers **2A2**
　　box office **2A2**

dept. store **2A2**
drug store **2A2**
front office **2A2**
grocery store **2A2**
restaurant **2A2**
Catalogers, library **4B1**
Caterers **3B7**
Catholic (Roman) priests **12B3**
Cattle dehorners **15B5**
Cement masons **6B3**
Cementing (gluing) machine ops.
　and tenders **1D22**
Central office craft occs.,
　telephone industry **9A1**
Central office equipment in-
　stallers, telephone industry **9A2**
Ceramic engineers **8B4**
Chauffeurs, private **3D1**
Checkers:
　　car **2A11**
　　credit **2A18**
　　in drafting **8G2**
　　photo **1D14**
　　policy **2A11**
　　shipping **2A11**
Chefs **3B2**
　　train **7C4**
Chemical engineers **8B5**
Chemical equip. controllers and
　ops. **1D23**
Chemical mixers, in photo
　labs **1D14**
Chemical oceanographers **8C4**
Chemical plant and system ops.
　1D24
Chemical technicians **8G3**
Chemists **8F2/8B5**
　　quality control **8B5**
Chief cooks (MM) **7B2**
Chief engineers, broadcasting **8G1**
Chief engineers (MM) **7B1**
Chief mates (MM) **7B1**

Chief stewards (MM) **7B2**
Children's librarians **4B1**
Chiropractors **10B1**
Church musicians **13A3**
Circulation clerks, library **4B2**
Circus ops. and wkrs. **14B7**
City managers **2E5**
    deputy **2E5**
City planners **2E16**
Civil engineering technicians **8G3**
Civil engineers **8B6**
Claim:
    adjusters, insurance **2D2**
    examiners, insurance **2D2**
    representatives, insurance **2D2**
Claims takers **2E18**
Classical musicians **13A3**
Classification clerks **2A11**
Classifiers, library **4B1**
Cleaners **3A1**
Cleaning and related occs. **3A**
Clergy **12B**
Clerical wkrs., mining industry **16A8**
Clerk typist **2A13**
Clerks:
    account **2A1**
    actuarial **2A11**
    adjustment **2E19**
    assignment **2A11**
    bank **2C1**
    brokerage **5A11**
    checkout **2A2**
    classification **2A11**
    coding **2A11**
    court **2A14**
    credit **2A18**
    demurrage **2A11**
    desk **2A5**
    exchange **2C1**
    file **2A4**
    hotel front office **2A5**

interest **2C1**
inventory **2A12**
licensing **2A19**
loan **2A18**
mail **2A16**
medical record **10C5**
mortgage processing
    2A13/2C1
municipal **2A17**
new account **2C1**
order **2A20**
personnel **2A11**
postal **2A7**
posting **2A11**
procurement **2A12**
real estate **2A15**
receiving and/or
    shipping **2A10**
reconcilement **2C1**
reservation **2A5**
room **2A5**
shipping and/or receiving
    2A10
statement **2C1**
statistical **2A11**
stock **2A12**
supply **2A12**
traffic **2A10**
transit **2C1**
Climatologists **8C3**
Clinical:
    dietician **10F1**
    psychologist **11A6**
Clock repairers **9B22**
Coach, commercial sports **14A1**
Coach, non-commercial and
    amateur sports **14B8**
Coating (painting and decorating)
    wkrs. **1D30**
Coding clerks **2A11**
Collection workers **2A3**
Collectors:

Cooperative Extension:
    service workers **15C6**
    social workers **12C1**
Copy writers, advertising **2E2**
Coremakers **1A3**
Correction officers **3E1**
Correspondence school teachers **4A6**
Correspondent officers, in banks **2C2**
Cosmetologists **3C3**
Cosmetology school teachers **4A6**
Cost estimators **2E7**
Counseling:
    occs. **12A**
    psychologists **11A6**
Counselors:
    admissions **2E6**
    career planning **2E6**
    college **2E6**
    college career planning **12A4**
    employment **12A2**
    rehabilitation **12A3**
    school **12A1**
Counter (food) wkrs. **3B4**
Court:
    clerks **2A14**
    reporters **2A9**
Cow testers **15B4**
Credit:
    checkers **2A18**
    clerks **2A18**
    managers **2E8**
Crew leaders, farm labor **15B10**
Crew schedulers **2A11**
Crop:
    dusters **15B8**
    reporters **15C4**
Crossing guards **3E15**
Curators:
    for museums **11A4**
    for private houses **3D1**

Custodians, building **3A1**
Customer:
    relations personnel **13C2**
    service personnel **13C2**
Customers' brokers, securities **5A11**
Customs inspector **3E10**
Cutters, in photo labs **1D14**

Dairy processing equip. ops. and tenders **1D25**
Dance instructors **14B19**
    aerobic **14B18**
Dance therapists **13A2**
Dancers **13A2**
Darkroom technicians **1D4**
Data processing school teachers **4A6**
Datatypists **2B1**
Dean of students **2E6**
Deck utility hands **7B2**
Decorating (painting and/or coating) workers **1D30**
Decorators:
    commercial **13B3**
    interior **13B6**
Dehorners, cattle **15B5**
Demurrage clerks **2A11**
Dental:
    assistants **10A2**
    laboratory technicians **10A4**
    hygienists **10A3**
Dentists **10A1**
Department store cashier **1D14**
Deputy:
    city managers **2E5**
    sheriff **3E13**
Derrick ops., oil and gas **16B9**
Design occs. **13B**

24

transmission, in broadcasting **8G1**

Engravers **1C7**

Environmental:
health inspectors **3E10**
scientists **8C**

Episcopal clergy **12B1**

Equipment:
farm, sales worker **15C9**
sporting, rental ops. and wkrs. **14B11**

Etchers **1C7**

Ethnologists **11A1**

Evaluation research psychologists **11A6**

Examiners:
polygraph **3E14**
title **5A12**

Exchange clerks **2C1**

Executive housekeepers **3A2**

Executive office holders **2E13**

Executives:
account **5A11**
advertising **2E2**

Experimental psychologists **11A6**

Exploration:
geophysicists **8C2**
offshore oil, occs. **16B7**
oil and gas, crews **16B1**

Explosives wkrs. **6B23**

Extension:
agricultural, agents **12C1**
service workers, cooperative **12C1**

Extractive metallurgical engineers **8B10**

FBI special agents **3E2**

Faculty, college and university **4A3**

Fallers, logging **8A2**

Farm:
equipment mechanics **9B10**
equipment sales workers **15C9**
hands **15A2**
labor contractors **15B10**
labor crewleaders **15B10**
labor supervisors **15A2**
laborers **15A2**
managers **15B7**
operators **15A1**
production occs. **15A**

Farmers:
tenant **15A2**
animal **15A4**
plant **15A3**

Farriers **1D3**

Fashion:
consultants **5A7**
designers **5A7**
models **5A7**

Fast food prep. and svc. **3B8**

Field technicians, broadcast **8G1**

File clerks **2A4**

Filling machine ops. **1D29**

Financial aid (for students) personnel **2E6**

"Finish" carpenters **6B2**

Finishers:
drywall **6B6**
furniture **1D27**
ophthalmic laboratory **1D13**

Finishing workers, construction **6A**

Fire protection engineers **3E11**

Firearms inspectors **3E10**

Firefighters **3E4**

Firers-Watertenders (MM) **7B2**

Fish farming **15D**

Fish hatchery workers **15F**

Fishery workers **15E**

Fitters, in industrial production **1D5**
Fitting models **5A7**
Flight attendants **7A4**
Floor covering installers **6B9**
Floral designers **13B4**
Florists **13B4**
Food:
    counter workers **3B4**
    inspectors **3E10**
    service occs. **3B**
    technologists **8G4**
Football:
    coaches and team owners,
        professional **14A1**
    players, professional **14A1**
Foreign:
    buyers **2E4**
    student advisors **2E6**
Foremen **1D4**
Forest nursery workers **5A15**
Foresters **8A1**
Forestry:
    pest controllers **3A3**
    technicians **8A2**
Forewomen **1D4**
Forge shop occs. **1D8**
Foundry occs. **1A**
Frame wirers, telephone industry **9A1**
Freelance:
    photographers **13B8**
    radio announcers **13C3**
    reporters **2A9**
    television announcers **13C3**
Front:
    -end mechanics **9B3**
    office cashiers **2A2**
    office clerks, hotel **2A5**
Funeral directors **3C4**
Furnace:
    installers **9B1**

operators and tenders **1D28**
Furniture:
    finishers **1D27**
    upholsterers **9B11**

Gang leader, in industrial and
    other blue-collar occs. **1D4**
Garbage men **3A4**
Gardeners:
    except private household **3F7**
    private household **3D1**
Gas (and oil):
    drilling personnel **16B2**
    exploration crews **16B1**
Gas:
    burner mechanics **9B1**
    dispatchers, statistical clerk **2A11**
    natural, processing person-
      nel **16B5**
Gasoline service station
    attendants **5A4**
Genealogists **11A4**
General:
    construction occs. **6A**
    contractor **6B5**
    houseworkers **3D1**
    millwrights **1D11**
    stenographers **2A9**
Geochemists **8C1**
Geochronologists **8C1**
Geodesists **8C2**
Geodetic surveyors **8G5**
Geographers **11A3**
    economic **11A3**
    physical **11A3**
    political **11A3**
    regional **11A3**
    urban **11A3**
Geological:

oceanographers **8C1/8C4**
technicians **8G3**
Geologists **8C1**
astro **8C1**
economic **8C1**
engineering **8C1**
petroleum **8C1**
Geomagneticians **8C2**
Geomorphologists **8C1**
Geophysical prospecting
surveyors **8G5**
Geophysicists **8C2**
exploration **8C2**
solid earth **8C2**
Geriatric aides **10D3**
Glaziers **6B10**
Gluing machine ops. and tenders
1D22
Golf:
course ops. and wkrs. **14B9**
instructor, or teacher **14B14**
player, professional **14A1**
tournament promoter **14A1**
Government:
accountants **2E1**
construction inspectors **3E7**
health and regulatory
inspectors **3E8**
Graders:
logging **8A2**
agricultural commodity
3E8/15C8
Graduate assistants **4A5**
Grain preparation services **15B9**
Graphic:
artists **13B2**
designers **13B2**
Grave diggers **6B11**
Grinders:
forge shop **1D8**
lens **1D13**
Grocery:

cashiers **2A2**
checkout clerks **2A2**
Groundskeepers:
except private household **3F7**
private household **3D1**
Guards:
crossing **3E15**
security **3E5**
Gunsmiths **1D9**
Gymnasium ops. and wkrs.:
membership **14B12**
non-membership **14B13**

Hair stylists **3C3**
Hammer-operators **1D8**
Hammersmiths **1D8**
Hand:
compositor, printing **1C1**
packers and packagers **1D35**
Hands:
deck (MM) **7B2**
farm **15A2**
utility (MM) **7B2**
Hatchery, fish, wkrs. **15F**
"Head" Housekeepers **3A2**
Health:
community nurses **10D1**
consultants, occ. **3E11**
inspectors, environmental
3E10
inspectors, government **3E10**
nurses, occ. **10D1**
occupations **10**
services administrators **10F3**
workers, occupational **3E11**
Heat treaters, in forge shops **1D8**
Heaters, in forge shops **1D8**
Heating:

(and air-conditioning/
    refrigeration)
    mechanics **9B1**
    and refrigeration technicians
    8G3
Helpers:
    cook, in private house-
      holds **3D1**
    surveying **8G5**
High-speed printer ops. **2B1**
Highway:
    construction workers **6B22**
    maintenance workers **6B25**
    patrol officers **3E8**
Historians **11A4**
Hockey, ice:
    coaches, professional
      14A1
    players, professional
      14A1
Home:
    curators, private **3D1**
    health (homemaker) aide
      10D3
Homemaker-home health aide
    10D3/12C2
Horse race track ops. and
    wkrs. **14A2**
Horticulturists **8D2**
Hospital:
    attendants **10D3**
    nurses **10D1**
Hosts and hostesses, restaurant
    3B9
Hotel:
    assistants **2E9**
    front office clerks **2A5**
    housekeepers **3A2**
    housekeepers assistants **3A2**
    managers **2E9**
Household:
    private, service occs. **3D**

private, workers **3D1**
Houseworkers, general **3D1**
Housing (student) officers **2E6**
Hunters **15G**
Hydrologic technicians **8G3**
Hydrologists **8C2**
Hygienists:
    dental **10A3**
    industrial **3E9**

Ice hockey players, coaches and
    owners, professional **14A1**
Immigration inspectors, govern-
    ment **3E10**
Income maintenance workers
    12C3
Indexers **2E22**
Industrial:
    designers **13B5**
    engineers **8B8**
    hygienists **3E11**
    machinery repairers **9B12**
    nurses **10D1**
    photographers **13B8**
    production occs. **1**
    production technicians **8G3**
    psychologists **11A6**
    sales workers **5A6**
Information:
    public, officer **13C2**
    science specialists **4B1**
Inhalation therapy workers **10C9**
Inseminators, artificial, in farm
    animals **15B3**
Inspectors:
    agricultural quarantine
      (government) **3E10**
    air safety (government) **3E10**
    alcohol, tobacco and fire-
      arms (government) **3E10**
    building (government) **3E9**

Keypunch operators **2B1**
Kiln operators and tenders **1D28**
Kindergarten teachers **4A2**

LPNs (licensed practical nurses)
　10D2
LVNs (licensed vocational nurses
　10D2
Labor, farm:
　contractors **15B10**
　supervisors **15A2**
Labor relations:
　specialist **2E12**
　workers **2E12**
Laboratory:
　color, technicians **1D14**
　dental, technicians **10A4**
　medical, assistants **10C4**
　medical, technicians **10C4**
　medical, workers **10C4**
　ophthalmic, technicians
　　1D13
　photofinishing, workers
　　1D14
　photographic, occs. **1D14**
Laborers:
　construction **6B4**
　farm **15A2**
Land surveyors **8G5**
Landscape architects **13B7**
Lathers **6B14**
Launderers, private **3D1**
Lawyers **2E10**
Layout workers **1D5**
Legal secretaries **2A9**
Legislators **2E13**
Lens grinder, ophthalmic **1D13**
Librarians **4B1**
　acquisition **4B1**

children's **4B1**
community outreach **4B1**
computer tape **2B1**
in private homes **3D1**
public **4B1**
school **4B1**
special **4B1**
special collection **4B1**
young adult **4B1**
Library:
　aides **4B2**
　assistants **4B2**
　automation specialists **4B1**
　clerks **4B2**
　occs. **4B**
　technicians **4B2**
Licensed nurses:
　practical **10D2**
　vocational **10D2**
Licensing clerks **2A19**
Lie detection service personnel
　3E14
Life science occs. **8D**
Life scientists **8D2/15A7**
Lighting technicians, broadcasting
　8G1
Limnologists **8C4**
Line installers **9A3**
Linguistic anthropologists **11A1**
Linotype machine ops. **1C1**
Lithographers **1C2**
Loan:
　clerks **2A18**
　officers, in banks **2C2**
Lobby attendants **14B20**
Local:
　transit busdrivers **7D2**
　truckdrivers **7D3**
Locksmiths **9B14**
Locomotive engineers **7C6**
Log:
　graders **8A2**

handling equip. ops. **8A2**
scalers **8A2**
Logging tractor ops. **8A2**
Long-distance:
telephone ops. **3F3**
truckdrivers **7D4**
Loss control consultants **3E11**
Lutheran ministers **12B1**

Machine:
coremakers, in foundries **1A3**
molders, in foundries **1A2**
movers, ironworkers **6B13**
occs. **1B**
Machine ops.:
adding and calculating **2A6**
billing **2A6**
bookkeeping **2A6/2C1**
construction **6B15**
dictaphone **2A13**
duplicating **2A6**
electronic, various **2C1**
filling **1D29**
linotype **1C1**
mail handling **2A6**
mail preparing **2A6**
office **2A6**
packaging **1D29**
proof **2C1**
soldering **1D33**
tabulating **2A6**
textile **1D32**
transcribing **2A13**
woodworking **1D34**
word processing **2A13**
Machine tool:
operators **1B3**
set-up workers **1B4**
Machinery maintenance wkrs.
9B27

Machinists:
all-round **1B1**
railroad shop **7C7**
Magazine:
publishers **13C6**
stand ops. and wkrs. **5A9b**
Magistrates **3E6**
Magnetic-tape typewriter ops.
2A13
Maids, private **3D1**
Mail:
carriers **3F1**
clerks **2A16**
handling machine ops. **2A6**
preparing machine ops. **2A6**
Maintainers, railroad signals **7C8**
Maintenance:
electricians **10B15**
income wkrs. **12C3**
mechanics **10B12**
men, elevator **6B8**
personnel, oil well **16B4**
technicians, broadcasting **8G1**
Management:
assistants **2E5**
consultants **2E21**
trust officers **2C2**
Management accountants:
industrial **2E1**
private **2E1**
Managers:
account **2E1**
bank **2C2**
branch, bank **2C2**
building **2E20**
city **2E5**
credit **2E8**
deputy city **2C5**
hotel **2E9**
merchandise **2E4**
range **8A3**
Manufacturers':

agents **5A6/5A14**
representatives **5A6/5A14**
sales wkrs. **5A6/5A14**
Manufacturing inspectors **1D10**
Marble setters **6B1**
Marine surveyors **8G5**
Market research wkrs. **2E11**
Masons:
    brick and stone **6B1**
    cement **6B3**
Masters (MM) **7B1**
Materials scientists **8B10**
Mates, chief and 3rd (MM) **7B1**
Mathematics occs. **8E1**
Meatcutters **3B5**
Mechanical:
    engineering technicians **8G3**
    engineers **8B9**
    inspectors **3E9**
    instrument makers **1B2**
    metallurgists **8B10**
    workers **6A**
Mechanics:
    air-conditioning and refrigeration **9B1**
    airplane **7A2**
    auto glass **9B4**
    auto radiator **9B4**
    automobile **9B4**
    boat-engine **9B5**
    bowling-pin machine **9B6**
    brakes **9B4**
    bus **9B20b**
    elevator **6B8**
    farm equipment **9B10**
    front end **9B4**
    gas burner **9B1**
    heating **9B1**
    maintenance **9B12**
    motorcycle **9B16**
    occs. **9**
    oil burner **9B1**

    truck **9B20a**
    tune-up **9B4**
    vending machine **9B21**
Media specialists, in libraries **4B1**
Medical:
    anthropologists **9A1**
    geographers **9A3**
    lab assistants **10C4**
    lab workers **10C4**
    microbiologists **8D2**
    practitioners occs. **10B**
    record, administrators **10F4**
    record, technicians and clerks
        10C4
    secretaries **2A9**
    technicians **10C4**
    technicians, emergency **10C3**
    technologist occs. **10C**
Membership:
    secretaries **2A9**
    sports and rec. club ops. and
        wkrs. **14B12**
Merchandise:
    displayers **13B3**
    managers **2E4**
Merchant Marine:
    occs. **7B**
    officers **7B1**
    sailors **7B2**
Mess attendants (MM) **7B2**
Metal patternmakers, in foundries
    1A1
Metallurgical engineers **8B10**
Metallurgists, mechanical **8B10**
Meteorological technicians **8G3**
Meteorologists **8C2/8C3**
    physical **8C3**
    synoptic **8C3**
Meter:
    installers and repairers,
        electric **9B23**
    readers, public utilities **3F2**

Microbiologists **8D2**
   medical **8D2**
Millwrights **1D11/9B12**
Mine inspectors **3E10**
Mineralogists **8C1**
Mining:
   administrators **16A6**
   clerical wkrs. **16A8**
   engineers **8B11/16A7**
   inspectors **16A2**
   occs. **16A**
   operatives **16A1**
   professionals **16A7**
   shift boss **16A3**
   surveyors **16A9**
   technical personnel **16A9**
Ministers, Protestant **12B1**
Mixers, chemical, in photo labs **1D14**
Mobile home repairers **9B28**
Model dressers **13B3**
Models **5A7**
   artists' **5A7**
   fashion **5A7**
   fitting **5A7**
   photographic **5A7**
   showroom **5A7**
Molders, in foundries **1A2**
Monotype keyboard ops. **1C1**
Mortgage processing clerks, banks **2A13/2C1**
Motion picture projectionists **1D12**
Motorcycle:
   mechanics **9B16**
   parts counter wkrs. **5A1**
   race track ops. and wkrs. **14A2**
   sales workers **5A2**
   service advisors **5A3**
Mounters, automatic, in photo labs **1D14**

Municipal clerks **2A17**
Music:
   school teachers **4A6**
   therapists **13A3**
Musicians:
   church **13A3**
   "classical" **13A3**
   "folk" **13A3**
   instrumental **13A3**
   "jazz" **13A3**
   "popular" **13A3**
   vocal **13A3**

Natural gas processing personnel **16B5**
Neighborhood wkrs. **12C3**
New account clerks **2C1**
News, market, reporters **15C4**
Newsletter publishers **13C5**
Newspaper:
   publishers **13C5**
   reporters **13C1**
Non-commercial sports, coaches and managers **14B8**
Non-membership sports and rec. club ops. and wkrs. **14B13**
Nurse educators **10D1**
Nursery workers **5A15**
Nurses:
   community health **10D1**
   hospital **10D1**
   in private homes **3D1**
   industrial **10D1**
   licensed practical (LPN) **10D2**
   licensed vocational (LVN) **10D2**
   occ. health **10D1**
   office **10D1**
   private duty **10D1**

registered (RN) **10D1**
Nursing:
    aides **10D3**
    assistants **10D3**
    occs. **10D**
    school teachers **4A6**
    wkrs., auxiliary **10D3**
Nutritionists **10F1**

Occupational:
    safety and health wkrs. **3E11**
    therapists **10E1**
Occupational health:
    consultants **3E11**
    nurses **10D1**
Occupational therapy:
    aides **10E2**
    assistants **10E2**
Oceanographers **8C1/8C4**
    biological **8C4/8D2**
    chemical **8C4**
    geological **8C4/8C1**
    physical **8C4**
Oceanographic engineers **8C4**
Office:
    machine ops. **2A6**
    nurses **10D1**
    occs. **2**
    secretaries **2A9**
Office, central:
    craft occs., in telephone in-
        dustry **9A1**
    equipment installers,
        telephone industry **9A2**
Officers:
    bank **2C2**
    correction **3E1**
    correspondent **2C2**
    highway patrol **3E8**
    loan **2C2**
    (MM) **7B1**

operations **2C2**
police **3E7**
public information **13C2**
radio **7B1**
state police **3E8**
student housing **2E6**
trust management **2C2**
Offshore oil exploration **16B7**
Oil:
    burner mechanics **9B1**
    exploration, offshore **16B7**
Oil and gas:
    drilling personnel **16B2**
    exploration crews **16B1**
Oil well:
    maintenance personnel **16B4**
    operators **16B3**
Oilers **7B2**
Oilfield services personnel **16B6**
Operating:
    engineers **6B15**
    room technicians **10C6**
Operative builders **6B5**
Operatives, mining **16A1**
Operators:
    adding and calculating
        machine **2A6**
    amusement concessions and
        rides **14B2**
    amusement park **14B1**
    animal show **14B3**
    arcade **14B4**
    billiard and pool hall **14B5**
    billing machine **2A6**
    bookkeeping machine **2C1**
    bowling alley **14B6**
    brake **7C2**
    card-tape-converter **2B1**
    circus **14B7**
    color printer **1D14**
    computer **2B1**
    console **2B1**

construction machines **6B15**
dictaphone **2A13**
directory assistance **3F3**
duplicating machine **2A6**
electronic machine **2C1**
farm **15A1**
golf course **14B9**
hammer **1D8**
high speed printer **2B1**
jack-hammer **6B22**
keypunch **2B1**
linotype machine **1C1**
log-handling equip. **8A2**
long-distance **3F3**
machine tool **1B3**
magnetic tape typewriter **2A13**
mail handling machine **2A6**
mining preparation plant **16A4**
monotype keyboard **1C1**
office machine **2A6**
oil well **16B3**
(PBX) **3F3**
power truck **1D15**
press **1D8**
printing press **1C5**
professional sports club **14A1**
proof machine **2C1**
race track **14A2**
recreation services **14B10**
sporting goods and equip- ment rental **14B11**
sports and recreation club, membership **14B12**
sports and recreation club, non-membership **14B13**
sports arenas **14A1**
swimming pool **14B15**
tabulating machine **2A6**
telegraph **3F6**
telephone **3F3**

teletype **3F6**
tennis court **14B16**
ticket sales office **14B17**
tower **7C11**
transcribing machine **2A13**
wastewater treatment plant **1D18**
word processing machine **2A13**
Ophthalmic:
  dispensers **10F2**
  laboratory technicians **1D13**
Opticians, dispensing **10F2**
Optometric assistants **10C7**
Optometrists **10B2**
Order:
  clerks **2A20**
  fillers, wholesale and retail sales **2A21**
Orderlies **10D3**
Ordinary seamen **7B2**
Organ tuners and repairers **9B17**
  electronic **9B17**
  pipe **9B17**
Organizational psychologists **11A6**
Ornamental ironworkers **6B13**
Orthodox Jewish Rabbis **12B2**
Osteopathic physicians **10B3**
Outdoor advertising personnel **2E2**
Outreach:
  community, librarians **4B1**
  wkrs. **12C3**
Overseers **1D4**

PBX:
  installers and repairers **9A4**
  operators **3F3**
Packaging machine ops. **1D29**
Packers:

hand 1D35
produce 15A2
Painters 6B16
automobile 1D2
production 1D16
Painting (decorative and/or
coating) wkrs. 1D30
Paleo-magneticians 8C2
Paleontologists 8C1
Paperhangers 6B16
Paramedics (EMT) 10C3
Park, amusement, ops. and
wkrs. 14B1
Parking attendants 7D5
valet 7D5
Parts counter workers:
automobile 5A1
bus 5A1
motorcycle 5A1
RV 5A1
truck 5A1
Passenger agents 7A5
Pathologists 8D2
speech 10E5
Patternmaker 1A1
metal 1A1
wood 1A1
Pavers, streets and roads 6B22
Payroll clerks 2A11
Performing artists 13A
Personal:
attendants 3D1
service occupations 3C
Personality psychologists 10A6
Personnel:
clerks 2A11
college student, wkrs. 2E6
recruiters 2E12
wkrs. 2E12
Pest controllers 3A3
forestry 3A3
Petroleum:

engineers 8B12
geologists 8C1
occs. 16B
refining occs. 16C
Pharmacists 10F5
Pharmacologists 8D2
Photo:
assemblers 1D14
checkers 1D14
Photoengravers 1C3
Photofinishing lab workers 1D14
Photograph retouchers 1D14
Photographers 13B8
commercial 13B8
freelance 13B8
industrial 13B8
portrait 13B8
Photographic:
laboratory occs. 1D14
models 5A7
Photojournalists 13B8
Phototypesetters 1C1
Physical:
anthropologists 11A1
geographers 11A3
meteorologists 8C3
oceanographers 8C4
scientists 8F
therapists 10E3
Physical therapy:
aides 10E4
assistants 10E4
Physicians 10B4
osteopathic 10B3
Physicists 8F3
"astro" 8F1
Physiological psychologists 11A6
Physiologists 8D2
Piano:
technicians 9B17
tuners and repairers 9B17
Picklers, in forge shops 1D8

natural gas, personnel 16B5
word, machine ops. and
    supervisors 2A13
Procurement clerks 2A12
Produce:
    packers 15A2
    sorters 15A2
Production:
    farm, occs. 15A
    painters 1D16
Production, industrial:
    engineering technicians 8G3
    occs. 1
Professional Agri-Business
    occs. 15C
Professional sports club:
    ops. 14A1
    players and other wkrs. 14A1
    promoters 14A1
Professionals, mining 16A7
Professors:
    college 4A4
    university 4A4
Programmers, computer 2B2
Projection printers 1D14
Projectionists, motion picture
    1D12
Promoters:
    professional sports club 14A1
    sports events 14A1
Proof:
    machine ops. 2C1
    readers 13C8
Prosecuting attorneys 3E12
Prospecting (geophysical) sur-
    veyors 8G5
Protection (fire) engineers 3E9
Protective service occs. 3E
Protestant ministers 12B1
Psychiatric aides 10D3
Psychologists 11A6
    clinical 11A6

community 11A6
comparative 11A6
consumer 11A6
counseling 11A6
developmental 11A6
educational 11A6
engineering 11A6
environmental 11A6
evaluation research 11A6
experimental 11A6
industrial 11A6
organizational 11A6
personality 11A6
physiological 11A6
population 11A6
psychometric 11A6
school 11A6
social 11A6
Psychometric psychologists 11A6
Public:
    administrators 2E17
    information officers 13C2
    librarians 4B1
    relations wkrs. 13C2
    works inspectors 3E9
Public school teachers:
    college and university 4A4
    kindergarten and elementary
        4A2
    secondary 4A3
Publishers:
    book 13C7
    magazine 13C6
    newsletters 13C5
    newspapers 13C5
Purchasing agents 2E14
Pursers 7B1

Quality control chemists 8B5/8F7
Quarantine inspectors, agri-
    cultural 3E8

RNs **10D1**
RV:
    parts counter workers **5A1**
    sales workers **5A2**
    service advisors **5A3**
Rabbis **12B2**
    reform **12B2**
Race track ops. and wkrs. **14A2**
Radiator, auto, mechanics **9B4**
Radio:
    announcers **13C3**
    officers (MM) **7B1**
    service technicians **9B19**
Radiological technicians **10C8**
Rail car repairers **9B29**
Railroad occs. **7C**
Range:
    conservationists **8A3**
    ecologists **8A3**
    managers **8A3**
    scientists **8A3**
Real estate:
    agents and brokers **5A8**
    appraisers **5A8**
    assessors, for tax purposes
      2E3
    clerks **2A15**
Receiving clerks **2A10**
Receptionists **2A8**
Reconcilement clerks **2C1**
Record, medical:
    administrators **10F4**
    technicians and clerks **10C5**
Recording technicians **8G1**
    video **8G1**
Recreation clubs ops. and wkrs.:
    membership **14B12**
    non-membership **14B13**
Recreation occs. **14B**
Recreation services ops. and
    wkrs. **14B10**
Recreational vehicle:

parts counter wkrs. **5A1**
sales wkrs. **5A2**
service advisors **5A3**
Recruiters, personnel **2E12**
Refrigeration:
    engineers (MM) **7B2**
    mechanics **9B1**
    technicians **8G3**
Refuse collectors **3A4**
Regional:
    geographers **11A3**
    planners **2E16**
Registered:
    nurses **10D1**
    representatives, security sales
      5A11
Registrar personnel, for college
    students **2E6**
Regulatory inspectors,
    government **3E10**
Rehabilitation:
    counselors **12A3**
    occs. **10E/12A3**
Reinforcing ironworkers **6B13**
Relations, labor:
    specialists **2E12**
    wkrs **2E12**
Relations, public, wkrs. **13C2**
Rental, sporting goods and equip-
    ment, ops. and wkrs. **14B11**
Repair workers, streets and
    roads **6B22**
Repairers **9A and B**
    appliance **9B2**
    auto body **9B3**
    burgler alarm **3F5**
    business machines **9B7**
    car, train **7C7**
    central office, telephone **9A1**
    clock **9B22**
    electric sign **9B9**
    industrial machinery **9B12**

machinery, industrial **9B12**
organ, pipe and electric **9B17**
PBX **9A4**
piano **9B17**
shoe **9B18**
telephone **9A4**
watch **9B22**
Reporters:
    court **2A9**
    crop **15A4**
    freelance **2A9**
    newspapers **13C1**
Representatives:
    insurance claim **2D2**
    manufacturers' **5A6/5A14**
    registered, security sales
        5A11
    sales **5A6/5A14**
Research:
    dieticians **10F1**
    market, wkrs. **2E11**
    psychologists **11A6**
Reservation:
    agents, air transporta-
        tion **7A5**
    clerks, hotel **2A5**
Respiratory therapy wkrs. **10C9**
Restaurant:
    cashiers **2A2**
    hosts and hostesses **3B9**
Retail book store ops. and wkrs.:
    (new books) **5A9a i**
    (used books) **5A9a ii**
Retail trade sales wkrs. **5A9**
Retouchers, photograph **1D14**
Revenue agents **2E15**
Riggers:
    ironworkers **6B13**
    ships and theaters, etc. **9B30**
Road repair workers **6B22**
Roman Catholic Priests (diocesan
    and religious) **12B3**

Roofers **6B19**
"Rough" carpenters **6B2**
Roustabouts **16B8**
Route drivers **5A10**

Safety:
    air, inspectors **3E10**
    consumer, inspectors **3E10**
    engineers **3E11**
    occ., wkrs. **3E11**
Sailors (MM) **7B2**
Salary and wage administrators
    2E12
Sales:
    engineers **5A6**
    occs. **5**
    representatives **5A6/5A14**
    ticket, office ops. and wkrs.,
        sports and rec. events
        14B17
Sales wkrs.:
    automobile **5A2**
    farm equipment **15C9**
    industrial **5A6**
    manufacturers **5A6/5A14**
    retail **5A9**
    security **5A11**
    wholesale trade **5A14**
Sandblasters **1D8**
Sanitary engineers **3A4**
Scalers, logging **8A2**
Schedulers, crew **2A11**
School:
    agricultural, teachers **15C5**
    counselors **12A1**
    librarians **4B1**
    psychologists **11A6**
    secretaries **2A9**
School teachers:
    elementary **4A1**

kindergarten **4A1**
secondary **4A2**
specialized **4A4**
Science:
  life, occs. **8D**
  technicians **8G3**
Scientific occs. **8**
Scientists:
  animal **8D2**
  environmental **8C**
  life **8D2/15A7**
  materials **8A10**
  physical **8F**
  political **11A5**
  range **8A3**
  social **11**
  soil **8D3**
Seamen:
  able (MM) **7B2**
  ordinary (MM) **7B2**
Second hand **1D4**
Secondary school teachers **4A3**
Secretarial school teachers **4A6**
Secretaries:
  administrative **2A9**
  legal **2A9**
  medical **2A9**
  membership **2A9**
  office **2A9**
  private household **3D1**
  school **2A9**
  technical **2A9**
Secular priests, Roman Catholic **12B3**
Security:
  guards **3E5**
  sales wkrs. **5A11**
Seismologists **8C2**
Semiconductor, electronic, processors **1D26**
Senior:
  drafters **8G2**

typists **2A13**
Service:
  food, occs. **3B**
  occs. **3**
  private household, occs. **3D**
  protective, occs. **3E**
  station, gasoline, attendants **5A4**
Service advisors:
  automobile **5A3**
  motorcycle **5A3**
  RV **5A3**
  truck **5A3**
Services, personal **3C**
Set-up workers, machine **1B4**
Setters, marble **6B1**
Sewage plant ops. and wkrs. **1D18**
Sheetmetal wkrs. **6B20**
  train **7C7**
Sheriff **3E13**
  deputy **3E13**
Shift boss, mining **16A3**
Ship (MM):
  carpenters **7B2**
  electricians **7B2**
Shipping:
  checkers **2A11**
  clerks **2A10**
Shoe repairers **9B18**
Shop trade workers, train **7C7**
Shorthand reporters **2A9**
"Shotblasters" **1D8**
Showcase trimmers **13B3**
Showroom models **5A7**
Shuttle bus ops. **7D7**
Sign, electric, repairers **9B9**
Signal department workers, train **7C8**
Singers **13A3**
Sinkers, die **1D8**
Small engine specialists **9B31**

Soccer players, professional **14A1**
Social:
    psychologists **11A6**
    scientists **11**
    wkrs. **12C4**
Social service:
    aides **12C3**
    occs. **12**
Sociologists **11A7**
Soil:
    conservationists **8A4**
    scientists **8D3**
Soldering machine ops. **1D33**
Solid earth geologists **8C2**
Sorters, in banks **2C1**
Special:
    agents, F.B.I. **3E3**
    collection librarians **4B1**
    librarians **4B1**
Special trade contractors **6B5**
Specialists:
    academic **4B1**
    agricultural marketing **15C2**
    automatic transmission **9B4**
    automobile air-condition-
      ing **9B4**
    information science **4B1**
    labor-relations **2E12**
    library automation **4B1**
    media **4B1**
Speciality advertising service
  wkrs. **2E2**
Speech pathologists **10E5**
Splicers, telephone cable **9A3**
Sporting goods and equipment
  rental ops. and wkrs. **14B11**
Sports:
    arena ops. and wkrs. **14A1**
    club ops., promoters and
      wkrs., professional **14A1**
    instructors and teachers
      14B14

Sports club ops. and wkrs.:
    membership **14B12**
    non-membership **14B13**
Sports occs. **14**
    commercial **14A**
State:
    Highway Patrol officers **3E8**
    Police officers **3E8**
    agents, train **7C9**
Statement clerks **2C1**
Stationary engineers **1D17**
Statistical clerks **2A11**
Statisticians **8E2**
Stenographers:
    general **2A9**
    technical **2A9**
Stereotypers, in printing **1C4**
Stewardesses:
    airplane **7A4**
    train **7C10**
Stewards:
    airplane **7A4**
    chief (MM) **7B2**
    train **7C10**
Stock:
    brokers **5A11**
    car drivers **14A2**
    clerks **2A12**
Stonemasons **6B1**
Stratigraphers **8C1**
Strawboss **1D4**
Street:
    construction wkrs. **6B22**
    repair wkrs. **6B22**
Streetcar ops. **7D8**
Structural:
    ironworkers **6B13**
    wkrs., in construction **6A**
Student:
    activities personnel **2E6**
    college, personnel wkrs. **2E6**
    financial aid personnel **2E6**

44

Tracers (in drafting) **8G2**
Track workers, train **7C12**
Tractor ops. (logging) **8A2**
Trade:
    (retail) sales wkrs. **5A9**
    school teachers **4A6**
    (special) contractors **6B5**
    (wholesale) sales wkrs. **5A14**
Trades (shop) train **7C7**
Traffic:
    air, controllers **7A1**
    clerks **2A10**
Traffic engineers **8B13**
    assistant **8B13**
Train:
    bartenders **7C1**
    blacksmiths **7C7**
    boilermakers **7C7**
    brake ops. **7C2**
    car repairers **7C7**
    conductors **7C3**
    cooks and chefs **7C4**
    dining car attendants and
        dishwashers **7C5**
    electrical wkrs. **7C7**
    locomotive engineers **7C6**
    machinists **7C7**
    sheet metal wkrs. **7C7**
    shop trades **7C7**
    signal dept. wkrs. **7C8**
    station agents **7C9**
    stewards and stewardesses
        7C10
    telegraphers, telephoners and
        tower ops. **7C11**
    track wkrs. **7C12**
Transcribing machine ops. **2A13**
Transformer repairers **9B24**
Transit:
    busdrivers, local **7D2**
    clerks, bank **2C1**
Transmission:

    automatic specialists **9B4**
    engineers **8G1**
Transmitter technicians **8G1**
Transportation occs. **7**
Trapping **15H**
Travel agents **5A13**
Treaters, heat, forge shop **1D8**
Treatment, water, plant ops.
   1D18
Tree trimers (for public utilities)
   3F4
Trimmers:
    forge shop **1D8**
    showcase **13B3**
    tree (for public utilities) **3F4**
Trolley ops. **7D8**
Truck:
    mechanics **9B20a**
    parts counter wkrs. **5A1**
    power, ops. **1D15**
    sales wkrs **5A2**
    service advisors **5A3**
Truckdrivers:
    local **7D3**
    long-distance **7D4**
Trust management officers **2C2**
Tune-up mechanics **9B4**
Tuners:
    organ **9B17**
    piano **9B17**
Typewriter (magnetic-tape)
   ops. **2A13**
Typists **2A13**
    clerk **2A13**
    data **2B1**
    intermediate **2A13**
    junior **2A13**
    senior **2A13**
    -vari **2A13**

Underwriters (insurance) **2D3**
Unemployment claims takers
  2E18
United Methodist ministers **12B1**
University faculty:
  private **4A4**
  public **4A4**
University professors **4A4**
Upholsterers, furniture **9B9**
Upholstery repairers,
  automotive **9B9**
Upsetters, forge shop **1D8**
Urban:
  anthropologists **11A1**
  geographers **11A3**
  planners **2E16**
Ushers **14B20**
Utility hands (in MM) **7B2**
  deck (in MM) **7B2**

Varitypists **2A13**
Vending machine mechanics **9B21**
Veterinarians **8D2/10B6/15B1**
Video technicians:
  control **8G1**
  recording **8G1**
Vocal musicians **13A3/13A4**
Vocalists **13A3/13A4**
Vocational:
  counselors **12A2**
  (licensed) nurses **10D2**
  school teachers **4A6**
Volcanologists **8C1**

Wage and salary administrators
  2E12

Wage-hour compliance inspectors
  3E10
Waiters and waitresses **3B6**
Wastewater treatment plant
  operators **1D18**
Watch repairers **9B22**
Water tenders (in MM) **7B2**
Welders **1D19**
Welfare wkrs. **12C1-5**
Wholesale:
  distributors **5A14**
  specialty advertising service
    wkrs. **2E2**
  trade sales wkrs. **5A14**
Window dressers **13B3**
Wirers (frame, in central office
  telephone work **9A1**
Wood patternmakers (in
  foundries) **1A1**
Woodworking machine ops. **1D34**
Word processing machine:
  ops. **2A13**
  supervisors **2A13**
Writers:
  advertising copy **2E2**
  insurance policy **2A13**
  technical **13C4**

X-ray technicians **10C8**

Young adult librarians **4B1**

Zoologists **8D2**

Occupations Outline

Abbreviations:
> esp. *especially*
> incl. *including*
> mfg. *manufacturing*

1. Industrial Production and Related Occupations

A. Foundry Occupations

1. *Patternmakers* (incl. Metal patternmakers and Wood pattern-makers): 33s, 356s, 37s, 38s.

2. *Molders* (incl. Machine molders, Bench molders and Floor molders): 33s, 354s, 37s.

3. *Coremakers* (incl. Bench coremakers, Floor coremakers and Machine coremakers): 33s, 356s, 37s.

B. Machine Occupations

1. *(All-round) Machinists*: 20s, 22s, 28s, 33s, 34s, 35s, 36s, 37s, 76s.

2. *Instrument makers (mechanical)*: 38s, 738s, 873s.

3. *Machine tool operators*: 34s, 35s, 36s, 37s, 76s.

4. *Setup workers (machine tools)*: 34s, 35s, 37s.

5. *Tool-and-die makers*: 35s, 37s.

C. Printing Occupations

1. *Compositors* (incl. Hand compositors, Linotype machine operators, Monotype keyboard operators and Phototypesetters): 27s, 60s, 63s, 64s, 73s (+ manufacturers and government agencies that do their own printing).

2. *Lithographers*: 27s (and U.S. Government printing plants).

3. *Photoengravers*: 27s (esp. 275s) and Federal Government.

4. *Electrotypers and stereotypers*: 27s.

5. *Printing press operators and assistants*: 27s, 60s, 63s, 64s (+ manufacturers and government agencies that do their own printing).

6. *Bookbinders and bindery workers*: 27s, (esp. 278s), 823s and Federal Government.

7. *Etchers and engravers*: 275s, 347s, 308s.

47

D. Other Industrial Production and Related Occupations

1. *Assemblers*: 23s, 34s, 35s (esp. 357s), 36s, 37s, 721s.

2. *Automobile painters*: 41s, 421s, 551s, 753s.

3. *Blacksmiths* (incl. Farriers): 027s, 10–14s, 33s–35s, 40s, 769s, 794s.

4. *Blue-collar worker supervisor* (incl. Foreman, Second hand, Boatswain, Overseer, Strawboss and Gang leader): 01–09s, 10–14s, 15–17s, 20–39s, 40–49s, 50–59s (also in many governmental agencies).

5. *Boilermaker occupations* (incl. Layout workers and Fitters): 15–17s, 29s, 331–332s, 40s, 44s, 49s (also: Navy shipyards and Federal powerplants).

6. *Boiler tenders*: 24s, 32s, 33s, 49s, 806s, 82s, 651s.

7. *Electroplaters*: 34s (esp. 347s), 36s, 37s (also used in maintenance at some Federal installations).

8. *Forge shop occupations* (incl. Hammersmiths, Hammer operators, Press operators, Upsetters, Heaters, Inspectors, Die sinkers, Trimmers, Grinders, Sandblasters [or "shotblasters"], Picklers and Heat treaters): 34s (esp. 342s and 346s), 35s and 37s (esp. 371s and 372s).

9. *Gunsmiths*: 348s and 769s.

10. *Inspectors* (manufacturing): in general: 20–39s (esp. 22s, 23s, 25s, 31s, 35s, 36s). Also see: Forge shop occupations

11. *Millwrights* in general: 20–39s (esp. 24s, 26s, 28s, 34s, 35s, 37s). Also 15s, 16s, 17s.

12. *Motion picture projectionists*: 483s, 78s (esp. 781s and 783s), 792s, 82s (esp. 822s). Also large companies in the 20–39s.

13. *Ophthalmic laboratory technicians* (incl. Surfacer [Lens grinder] and Bench technician [Finisher]): 385s, 599s, 801s, 804s.

14. *Photographic laboratory occupations* (incl. Darkroom technicians, Color-lab technicians, Developers, Print washers, Projection printers, Photograph retouchers, Photofinishing laboratory workers, Color-printer operators, Print controllers, Automatic print developers, Cutters, Chemical mixers, Automatic mounters and Photo checkers and assemblers): 271s, 272s, 722s, 731s, 733s, 739s, 899s. Also, large companies in the 20–39s and some governmental agencies with photo labs.

15. *Power truck operators*: Groups 10–14, 20–39 (esp. 24s, 26s, 32s, 33s, 34s, 35s, 37s). Also 401s, 417s, 42s, 431s, 446s, 458s.

16. *Production painters*: 24s, 25s, 34s, 35s, 37s (esp. 371s, 372s), 39s.

17. *Stationary engineers*: 24s, 26s, 32s, 33s, 49s (esp. 491s, 493s, 494s, and 495s), 651s, 701s, 806s.

18. *Wastewater treatment plant operators* (Sewage plant operators): 20–39s that have wastewater treatment plants, 4941s, 495s (also Municipal plants and some Federal installations).

19. *Welders*: 13s, 15s, 16s, 17s, 34s, 35s, 36s, 37s, 38s, 39s, 46s, 75s, 76s.

20. *Bakers* (manufacturing): 205s.

21. *Cannery workers*: 201s, 203s, 209s.

22. *Cementing and gluing machine operators and tenders*: 138s, 15–179s, 20–209s, 24–28s and 30–39s.

23. *Chemical equipment controllers and operators*: primarily 281s. Also, some 283s.

24. *Chemical plant and system operators*: Mostly 28s.

25. *Dairy processing equipment operators and tenders*: 202s.

26. *Electronic semiconductor processors*: 367s.

27. *Furniture finishers*: 764s, 571s, 593s, 251s and 253s.

28. *Furnace and kiln operators and tenders*: Some in groups 28, 29 and 30. Also found in 242s, 321–323s and some in the 325–326s (esp. 325s).

29. *Packaging and filling machine operators*: 072s, 478s, 201–202s, 204–209s and group 21. 307s, 266s, 329s, 348s and 394s. (This is but a small sample of packaging machine jobs that can be found.)

30. *Painting, coating and decorating workers*: 25s, 321–326s, 364s, 391s, 273s and 311–319s.

31. *Power distributors and dispatchers*: 491s, 493s, 496s and some 33–35s.

32. *Textile machine operators*: 221–229s and some 231–239s.

33. *Soldering machine operators*: 34–37s, 75–76s, 152–179s, some 25s and possibly some 13s.

34. *Woodworking machine operators*: 242–249s, 251s, 252s, 253s, 254s and some 259s. Also some 764s.

35. Hand packers and packagers: 514s, 541s, 738s, 072s, 478s, 596s and some 53s and 54s. Also, some 201–209s and 321–326s.

2. Office Occupations

A. Clerical Occupations

1. *Bookkeeping workers* (incl. General bookkeeper and Account clerks): found in every major SIC group. An especially large number of bookkeepers work in the 50–59s. Also high are the 82s, 80s, 83s, 86s and 90–97s.

2. *Cashiers* (incl. Box office cashiers, Restaurant cashiers, Front office cashiers and Checkout clerks for grocery, department and drug stores, etc.): Cashiers work in most of the 52–59s. They are especially common in the 541s, 531s, 591s, 566s, 525s, 571s and 581s. They are also found in the 783s, 792s, 806s, 821s and 824s. Some cashiers work for government agencies, esp. in clubs, cafeterias and exchanges on military establishments (971 + specific retail SIC Code). Many cashier positions are part-time.

3. *Collection workers*: 602s, 603s, 61s, 732s. Many also work for major SIC groups 50–59.

4. *File clerks* (incl. Junior clerks): File clerks work in almost all SIC groups. A large percentage work in the 60s, 63s, 64s, 65s, 81s and 80s. Generally they gravitate toward major groups 60–97 (incl. most government agencies). There are many part-time and/or temporary positions in this field.

5. *Hotel front office clerks* (incl. Room or Desk clerks, Reservation clerks, etc.): 701 specifically and major group 70 in general.

6. *Office machine operators* (incl. Billing machine operators, Bookkeeping machine operators, Adding and Calculating machine operators, Mail preparing and Mail handling machine operators, Duplicating machine operators and Tabulating machine operators, etc.): Large numbers of Office machine operators work in the 60s, 63s, 64s and 50–59s. They are also employed in many other firms in the 60–97 groups. Large companies in the other SIC groups may also employ office machine operators.

7. *Postal clerks*: 431 (U.S. Government Post Office), 731s (Private postal services), 738s (Post Office contract stations).

8. *Receptionists*: A high percentage are found in the 80s (esp. 801s, 802s, 803s, 804s). Also found in the 805s, 806s, 808s, 809s. Large numbers work in the 63s, 64s, 60–62s, 20–39s and 70–89s. Also in any other SIC Code where the company has a front office that receives people.

9. *Secretaries and Stenographers* (incl. Administrative secretaries, Legal secretaries, Medical secretaries, Technical secretaries, Membership secretaries, School secretaries and regular, old-fashioned Office secretaries. Also incl. General stenographers, Technical stenographers, Shorthand reporters, Court reporters, and Free-lance reporters): 81s, 80s, 82s, 60s, 61s, 63–67s, 72–73s, 83s, 86s, 89s, 91–97s. Also found in most large companies from any of the other SIC groups. Many temporary and/or part-time positions.

10. *Shipping and receiving clerks* (incl. Traffic clerks): Found in most of the 20–39 groups. Also, many are employed in the 50–59 groups (esp. 50–51s).

11. *Statistical clerks* (incl. Shipping checkers, Car checkers, Talliers, Posting clerks, Classification clerks, Coding clerks, Personnel clerks, Payroll clerks, Actuarial clerks, Policy checkers, Demurrage clerks, Assignment clerks, Crew schedulers and Gas dispatchers): Most work in the 60–67s, 20–39s and 91–97s. However, they are found in almost all types of companies in every major SIC group.

12. *Stock clerks* (incl. Inventory clerks and Procurement clerks): Most

work in the 20–39s, 50–59s, 45s, 91–97s, 82s and 80s. They also work for any company that keeps large quantities of goods on hand — this might include any SIC group from 01–99.

13. *Typists* (incl. Junior typists, Intermediate typists, Senior typists, Clerk typists, Varitypists, Transcribing machine (dictaphone) operators, Policy writers (insurance), Mortgage processing clerks (banks), Magnetic-tape typewriter operators, Word processing machine operators and supervisors): Employed in all SIC groups (esp. 20–39s, 60–67s and 91–97s).

14. *Court clerks*: 921s.

15. *Real estate clerks*: 651s, 653s.

16. *Mail clerks*: Almost all SIC codes, esp. those companies and agencies receiving a large quantity of mail.

17. *Municipal clerks*: 91s.

18. *Credit checkers* (incl. Credit and Loan clerks): Many work in the 50–59s. Some work in the 20–39s, others in the 60–67s.

19. *Licensing clerks*: Mostly 91s and 92s. Also other government agencies in the 91–96 series.

20. *Order clerks*: 70–79s, 50–59s and 20–39s.

21. *Order fillers* (wholesale and retail sales): 50–59s.

22. *Dispatchers* (other): esp. 15–179s. Also 07s, 08s, 10–14s, 40–49s, 75–76s, 94–97s.

B. Computer and Related Occupations

1. *Computer operating personnel* (incl. Keypunch operators, Datatypists, Console operators, High-speed printer operators, Card-Tape converter operators and Tape librarians): Found in most SIC groups (esp. 20–39s, 50–59s, 60–64s, 73s and 91–97s).

2. *Programmers*: Mostly employed by the 20–39s, 60–64s, 73s (esp. 738s), 892s and 91–97s. Also employed by many large firms with their own expensive computer systems (ask to see a "Data Processing Index" or similar directory that lists what companies in your area have what computer systems).

3. *Systems analysts*: Many work for 20–39s, 60–64s, 737s (esp. 7374s). Also for 50–59s and 91–97s (or any company organization with a large data processing department).

C. Banking Occupations (and Other Credit Agencies)

1. *Bank clerks* (incl. Sorters, Proof-machine operators, Bookkeeping-machine operators, Reconcilement clerks, Transit clerks, New account clerks, Exchange clerks, Statement clerks, Interest clerks, Mortgage clerks, various Electronic machine operators, other clerical occupations unique to banking): 60s (esp. 602s) and 61s.

2. *Bank officers and managers* (incl. Loan officers, Trust management officers, Operations officers, Correspondent officers and Branch managers): 60s (esp. 602s) and 61s.

3. *Bank tellers*: 60s (esp. 602s) and 61s.

D. Insurance Occupations

1. *Actuaries*: 63s, 641s, 738s, 91–97s.

2. *Claim representatives* (incl. Claim adjusters and Claim examiners): 63s, 641s, 60s, 61s.

3. *Underwriters*: 63s (esp. 633s and 631s).

E. Administrative and Related Occupations

1. *Accountants* (incl. Public, Management [Industrial or Private] and Government accounting. Also incl. Controllers and Account managers): Most work for large firms headquartered in large cities (representing most all SIC Codes). Many are in the 893s and 91–97s (esp. 931s). Also some accountants teach full or part time (822s).

2. *Advertising executives* (and other advertising workers): incl. Advertising copy writers (899s), Advertising consultants and Advertising agency executives (731s). This heading also includes Aerial (731s), Billboard (731s) and other outdoor advertising personnel as well as specialty advertising service workers (for wholesalers): 519s. Advertising personnel are also employed in advertising departments of large companies that advertise (of almost any SIC Code).

3. *Assessors* (real and personal property — for tax purposes): 931s.

4. *Buyers* (incl. Foreign Buyers and Merchandise Managers): Mostly 52–59s.

5. *City managers* (incl. such Management assistants as Deputy city managers, Administrative assistants and Administrative analysts): Mostly 911s, some 912s or 913s. Also other 91–97s and some 738s.

6. *College student personnel workers* (incl. Dean of students, Admissions counselors, Registrar personnel, Student financial aid personnel, Career planning and placement counselors, Student activities personnel, College union staff, Student housing officers, Counselors and Foreign student advisors): 822s.

7. *Cost estimators* (found in all SIC Codes, esp. 20s–39s, 15–17s, 91–97s, 81–89s, 70–79s and 50–59s).

8. *Credit managers*: Many work in the 50–59s. Some work in the 20–39s, others in the 60–67s.

9. *Hotel managers and assistants*: 70s (esp. 701s).

10. *Lawyers*: Mostly 811s. Also 60–67s (esp. 661s), 91–97s, 47–49s, 20–39s, 83s (esp. 839s), 86s (esp. 866s) and other firms of varied SIC

Codes with a legal department or needing frequent legal services. Also, lawyers teach full or part-time in law schools (included in 822s).

11. *Market research workers*: Most are found in the 20–39s, 731s and 738s. Also, many work in the 52–59s, 792s and 271s. Others are employed by firms in the 892s and in various government planning agencies in the 91–97s.

12. *Personnel and labor relations workers* (incl. Personnel recruiters, Employment interviewers, Job analysts, Salary and wage administrators and Labor relations specialists): 20–39s, 60–64s, 45s (esp. 451s), 52–59s (esp. 531s), 736s, 91–97s (esp. 919s and 965s). Also 738s, 863s, 781s and 792s. Some teach related subjects in universities (822s).

13. *Politicians* (incl. Executive, Legislative and General): 91s.

14. *Purchasing agents*: 20–39s, 91–97s, 15–17s, 806s, 82s (esp. 821s and 822s).

15. *Tax collectors* (and Revenue agents): 931s.

16. *Urban and regional planners* (incl. City planners): Most work for 953s and 738s. Many work in other 95s and 96s (esp. 951s and 962s). Also, these types of planners work for 655s, 89s (esp. 892s) and 822s.

17. *Public administrators* (same as Politicians): 91s.

18. *Claims takers* (unemployment): 944s, possibly some 833s.

19. *Adjustment clerks* (mostly retail stores): 52–59s. Also some non-retail companies where necessary to adjust customer complaints.

20. *Building managers*: Some office and apartment buildings in the 651s. Also, some larger buildings of government agencies (91–97s), libraries (823s), schools (821 and 822s), hospitals (806s) and other medical buildings in 801–809s.

21. *Management consultants*: 738s and 874s.

22. *Abstractors, indexers and press-clipping service workers*: 738s and some 823s.

3. Service Occupations

A. Cleaning and Related Occupations

1. *Building custodians* (also known as Janitors or Cleaners): 651s, factories in the 20–39s, 82s, 80s, 78s and 79s. Some also work for 734s, 52–59s and 91–97s. Many Building custodians work only part time.

2. *Hotel housekeepers and assistants* (incl. Executive or "Head" housekeepers): 70s (esp. 701s).

3. *Pest controllers* (incl. Forestry pest controllers): Mostly 734s and 085s. A few Pest controllers work in the 91–97s.

4. *Sanitary engineers* (incl. Garbage men, Trash collectors and Refuse collectors): 421s, 495s and 951s.

B. Food Service Occupations

1. *Bartenders* (incl. Bartender helpers and Barmaids): 581s, 864s, 701s, 704s, 799s and some gambling establishments also in the 799s. There are many part-time positions available in this field.

2. *Cooks and chefs* (incl. Bakers): 581s, 701s, 82s (esp. 821s and 822s), 458s and 806s. Many Cooks also work in the 91–97s and in factories in the 20–39s. Also employing Cooks and Bakers are the 799s, 704s, 864s and some 881s.

3. *Dining room attendants and dishwashers*: Most work in the 581s and 7011s. Many dishwashers also work in the 82s (esp. 821s and 822s), 806s and some 91–97s. Many are part-time positions.

4. *Food counter workers*: 581s, some 591s and 82s (esp. 821s and 822s). Some 806s and 91–97s. Also, Food counter workers are found in some 783s as well as many of the 79s.

5. *Meatcutters*: 54s (esp. 541s and 542s). Also 51s (esp. 514s). Some Meatcutters work in the 581s, 701s, 806s and a few 91–97s.

6. *Waiters and waitresses*: Most work in the 581s. Some are found in the 701s, 822s and factories (with restaurant facilities) in the 20–39s group. They are also found in other 70s and in some 79s.

7. *Caterers*: 581s.

8. *Fast food preparation and service*: 581s.

9. *Restaurant hosts and hostesses*: 581s, 701s and 591s.

C. Personal Services

1. *Barbers*: Mostly 724s and 723s. Some work for 91–97s, 701s or 531s.

2. *Bellhops and bell captains*: 70s (mostly 701s).

3. *Cosmetologists* (incl. Beauty operators, Hairstylists and Beauticians): 723s, 724s and 531s. A few are employed by the 806s and 701s.

4. *Funeral directors and embalmers*: 726s (a few also work for hospitals [806s]).

5. *Porters* (baggage): 458s, 417s, 44s and 40s.

D. Private Household Service Occupations

1. *Private household workers* (incl. Domestic workers, General houseworkers, Maids, Day workers, Gardeners, Groundskeepers, Caretakers, Cooks, Cook helpers, Chauffers, Private nurses, Private secretaries, Private home curators or librarians, Launderers, Personal attendants, Companions, Babysitters and Butlers): 881.

E. Protective and Related Service Occupations

1. *Correction officers*: 922s (all levels of government).

2. *Detectives and detective agencies*: 738s.

3. *FBI special agents*: 922 (in resident agencies, field offices or in Bureau headquarters in Washington, D.C.).

4. *Firefighters* (incl. Fire dept. dispatchers): Most work in the 922s. Some work in fire departments on federal installations (91–97s), others in the 458s and large manufacturing plants (20–39s). Some Firefighters work in forestry services (085s).

5. *Guards* (security): 651s, 91–97s, 50–59s, 70s, 61–62s, 82s and 20–39s. Many Guards work for the 738s.

6. *Judges and magistrates*: 921 and 922s.

7. *Police officers* (incl. Police Dept. dispatchers): 922s.

8. *State police officers* (incl. State Highway Patrol officers): 922s — California has the largest, North Dakota the smallest and Hawaii doesn't have a State police force.

9. *Construction inspectors (government)* (incl. Building inspector, Electrical inspectors, Mechanical inspectors and Public works inspector): Mostly 953s and 951s.

10. *Health and regulatory inspectors (government)* (incl. Consumer safety inspectors, Food inspectors, Agricultural quarantine inspectors, Environmental health inspectors, Agricultural commodity graders, Immigration inspectors, Customs inspectors, Air safety inspectors, Mine inspectors, Wage-hour compliance inspectors and Alcohol, Tobacco and Firearms inspectors): 964s, 965s, 943s, 962s, 961s, 931s and possibly other codes in the 91–97s group.

11. *Occupational Safety and Health Workers* (incl. Safety engineers, Fire protection engineers, Industrial hygientists, Loss control and Occupational health consultants): Mostly in the 20–39s. Also in most large firms of many other SIC groups. Insurance companies (641s) sometimes employ Safety and Health workers.

12. *Prosecuting attorneys*: 922s.

13. *Sheriff* (incl. Deputy sheriff): 922s.

14. *Polygraph examiners* (incl. Lie detector service personnel): 738s and 92s.

15. *Crossing guards*: 821s, 15–17s, 919s, 922s and possibly some 401s and 96s.

F. Other Service Occupations

1. *Mail carriers*: 431.

2. *Meter readers*: (electric, gas, water or steam): 491s, 492s, 493s, 494s and 496s.

3. *Telephone operators* (incl. Long-distance operators, Directory assistance operators and PBX operators): 481s. Also in the 20–39s, 806s, 531s and other businesses.

4. *Tree trimmers* (for public utility lines): 078s.

5. *Alarm installers and repairers* (for burglar alarms): 173s and 738s.

6. *Telegraph operators* (incl. Teletype ops.): 482s, 20–39s, 806s, 531s and other businesses.

7. *Groundskeepers and gardeners* (except private household): 842s, 919s, 951s, 806s and some 82s (esp. 822s).

4. Education and Related Occupations

A. Teaching Occupations

1. *Preschool teachers*: 821s, some 835s and possibly some 829s.

2. *Kindergarten and elementary school teachers*: 821s (public and private).

3. *Secondary school teachers*: 821s (public and private).

4. *College and university faculty*: 822s (public and private).

5. *Graduate assistants*: 822s.

6. *Teachers in vocational, trade and other specialized, nonacademic (or nondegree granting) schools* (incl. Correspondence schools, Data processing schools, Business and secretarial schools, Nursing schools, Cosmetology schools, Art, music and drama schools, etc.): 824s and 829s.

7. *Teacher aides*: 821s (most work in public or private elementary schools – some work in public or private secondary schools).

8. *Audiovisual specialists*: All the 82s, esp. 821s and 822s.

B. Library Occupations

1. *Librarians*: (incl. Acquisitions librarians, Classifiers, Catalogers, Bibliographers, Special Collection librarians, Public librarians, Children's librarians, Community outreach librarians, Young adult librarians, School librarians, Media specialists, Academic specialists, Special librarians, Information science specialists and Library automation specialists): 823s, 821s and 822s. Librarians are also employed in the 941s, 922s, 971s, 806s and other private and governmental positions.

2. *Library technicians and assistants* (incl. Bookmobile drivers, Library clerks, Library aides and Circulation clerks): SIC Codes are basically the same as for Librarians.

5. Sales Occupations

A. Specific Sales Occupations

1. *Automobile parts counter worker* (incl. Motorcycle, truck, bus and RV parts): 551s, 553s, 556s, 557s and 559s. Also in the 501s, 593s

and possibly some 552s. Some parts counter workers are employed by 421s, 411s, 413s, 414s and 415s.

2. *Automobile sales workers* (incl. Motorcycles, trucks and RVs): 551s, 552s, 556s, 557s and 559s.

3. *Automobile service advisors* (incl. Motorcycle, truck and RV service advisors): Most work for large dealers in the 551s, 556s and 557s. Some work for 753s, 769s and 754s.

4. *Gasoline service station attendants*: 554s.

5. *Insurance agents and brokers*: 641s.

6. *Manufacturers' sales workers* (incl. Sales engineers, Industrial sales workers, Manufacturers' agents or representatives and some Sales reps.): 20–39s. More work in the 20s than any 2-digit code. Many also work in the 27s, 28s, 34s, 36s and 35s. Most Sales engineers work for the 35s, 37s, 34s and 38s. Many Manufacturers' agents and representatives are classified with wholesale distributors in the 50s and 51s.

7. *Models* (incl. Fashion models, Showroom or Fitting models, Photographic models and Artists' models): Mostly 736s. Also 22s and 23s, 513s. Some models work for 531s or 563s. Models also work in Modeling schools (829s), for Fashion designers (7399s) and beauty or Fashion consultants (738s). Models are also employed as Tour guides (799s).

8. *Real estate agents and brokers* (incl. Appraisers): 653s.

9. *Retail trade sales workers*: Mostly in the 531s, 533s, 539s, 56s and 54s. Also 596s. Retail trade sales workers also work for other firms in the 52–59 categories.

  a. Retail book store operators and workers
    i. New book stores: 594s.
    ii. Used book stores: 593s.
  b. Magazine and newspaper stand operators and workers: 599s.

10. *Route drivers*: Mostly 596s, 721s, 205s, 202s, 514s, 518s and other wholesale distributors in the 51s and 50s. Some Dairy farms (024s) employ Route drivers.

11. *Security sales workers* (incl. Registered representatives, Account executives or Customers' brokers, Stock brokers and Brokerage clerks): 62s (esp. 621s) and 63s. Also some 67s (esp. 672s).

12. *Title examiners*: 654s and 653s.

13. *Travel agents*: 472s (many Travel agents are self-employed).

14. *Wholesale trade sales workers* (incl. Wholesale distributors, Manufacturers' agents and representatives and some Sales representatives): Most are employed by firms in the 503s, 507s and 508s. Also, many work in the 514s, 512s, 511s, 513s, 501s and 506s. The rest of the wholesale SIC Codes (50–51) also employ sales workers.

15. *Nursery workers* (wholesale and retail): 519s, 018s and 526s. Also incl. Forest nursery workers (082s).

6. Construction Occupations

A. General Construction Occupations (incl. Structural workers, Finishing workers and Mechanical workers): 15s, 16s and 17s. Also some 10–14s and 20–39s. Some government agencies employ Construction workers (esp. 95–97s). Many Construction workers are self-employed.

B. Specific Construction Occupations
1. *Bricklayers, stonemasons and marble setters*: Mostly 17s and 15s. A few work for the 95–97s and possibly several other SIC Codes. Many are self-employed.
2. *Carpenters* (incl. "Rough" and "Finish"): Most work for 15s, 16s and 17s (esp. 175). Some work for organizations in the 95–97s, 49s, 20–39s or other large companies. Many are self-employed.
3. *Cement masons and terrazzo workers*: 16s, 15s and 17s (esp. 174s and 175s). Some work in the 49s, 95–97s and 20–39s.
4. *Construction laborers*: 15–17s, 95–97s and 49s.
5. *Contractors* (incl. General contractors, Operative builders and Special trade contractors): 15–17s.
6. *Drywall installers and finishers*: Mostly 174s. Also other contractors in the 15–17s groups.
7. *Electricians* (construction): Mostly 173s. Many are self-employed.
8. *Elevator constructors* (or mechanics, repairmen or maintenance men): Mostly 353s, 179s. Some work for firms in the 508s and others for government agencies (91–97s). Still others work for larger businesses that maintain and repair their own elevators.
9. *Floor covering installers*: Mostly 175s, 571s and the 15s (esp. 152s). Many are self-employed.
10. *Glaziers*: Mostly 179s and some 15s. A few work for 91–97s or businesses that do their own construction.
11. *Grave diggers*: 179.
12. *Insulation workers*: Mostly 174s and 179s. Some work for factories in the 20–39s or for large companies with their own cold-storage facilities.
13. *Ironworkers* (incl. Structural, Ornamental and Reinforcing ironworkers and Riggers and Machine movers): Mostly in the 154s, 162s and 179s.
14. *Lathers*: Mostly 174s (possibly some 399s: lath backing for plaster

display materials or scenery). Lathers sometimes work for general contractors in remodeling buildings of all types (152s or 154s).

15. *Operating engineers* (construction machine operators): 161s and 162s. Also many 49s (esp. 491s, 492s and 493s). Operating engineers work for many 20–39s and other businesses that do their own construction. Also, they work for state and local government public works and highway departments in the 95s and 96s and some sections of the federal defense industry (97s). Some work in mines (10–14s).

16. *Painters and paperhangers*: Mostly 172. Sometimes Painters and Paperhangers work for paint and paper-removal contractors (179s). Also, they may work directly for 152s and 154s. Some Maintenance Painters work for 701s, 651s, 20–39s and the 821s and 822s. Some municipal buildings maintenance departments employ Painters (734s or possibly 919s). Many Painters and Paperhangers are self-employed.

17. *Plasterers*. Mostly 174s. Also, some 152s and 154s.

18. *Plumbers, pipelayers and pipefitters*: Mostly 171s. Also, some 152s or 154s. Others work for 91–97s, 49s, 372s. Some do maintenance work for buildings (734s). Pipelayers and Pipefitters often work for 29s, 28s and 20s and esp. 162s.

19. *Roofers*: Mostly 176s. Some worked for businesses (no particular SIC Code) and government agencies (91–97s) that do their own construction and repair work. Many Roofers are self-employed.

20. *Sheet-metal workers*: Mostly 171s and 176s. Also, some 152s and 154s. Some work for businesses (no particular SIC Code) and government agencies (91–97s) that do their own construction and repair work.

21. *Tilesetters*: Mostly 174s. Also, some Tilesetters worked directly for contractors in the 154s.

22. *Highway and street construction workers* (incl. Jack-hammer operators, Pavers, Street repair workers, etc.): 161s.

23. *Blasters* (and explosives workers): Primarily 179s. Also found in 15–16s as well as some mining SIC Codes (10–14s). Public utilities (49s) and some government agencies (possibly 95–97s) use these workers.

24. *Acoustical carpenters*: 174s.

25. *Highway maintenance workers*: Primarily 161s. Also, some 458s.

26. *Cabinetmakers and bench carpenters*: 254s, 252s, 243s, 259s and possibly some 175s.

7. Occupations in Transportation Activities

A. Air Transportation Occupations
1. *Air Traffic Controllers*: Mostly 962s.
2. *Airplane mechanics*: 451s, 452s, 458s, 762s, 769s, 962s and 971s.

Also for large private companies of all types that operate their own planes for executives and cargo transportation.

3. *Airplane pilots*: 451s, 452s, 829s and 072s. Others work for large businesses that use their own airplanes to fly company cargo and executives. Also some 91–97s (esp. 971s).

4. *Flight attendants* (or "stewardesses" and "stewards"): Mostly 451s. Also some 452s.

5. *Reservation and passenger agents*: Mostly 451s. Also 452s.

B. Merchant Marine Occupations

1. *Merchant Marine officers* (incl. Captains, Masters, Chief mates, Third mates, Chief engineers, 1st, 2nd and 3rd assistant Engineers, Radio officers and Pursers): Mostly 441s. Also 442s and 443s.

2. *Merchant Marine sailors* (incl. Ordinary seamen, Able seamen, Boatswains, Deck utility hands, Ship carpenters, Wipers, Oilers, Firers-Watertenders, Ship electricians, Refrigeration engineers, Chief stewards, Chief cooks, Utility hands and Mess attendants): Mostly 441s. Also 442s and 443s.

C. Railroad Occupations

1. *Bartenders* (train): 401s and 404s.

2. *Brake operators*: 401s and 404s.

3. *Conductors*: 401s and 404s

4. *Cooks and chefs* (train): 401s and 404s.

5. *Dining car attendants and dishwashers* (train): 401s and 404s.

6. *Locomotive engineers: 401s and 404s.*

7. *Shop trades* (train—incl. Car repairers, Machinists, Electrical workers, Sheet-metal workers, Boilermakers and Blacksmiths): 401s and 404s.

8. *Signal department workers* (incl. Installers and Maintainers): 401s and 404s.

9. *Station agents*: 401s and 404s.

10. *Stewards and stewardesses* (train): 401s and 404s.

11. *Telegraphers, telephoners and tower operators*: 401s and 404s.

12. *Track workers*: 401s and 404s.

D. Driving Occupations

1. *Intercity bus drivers*: Mostly 411s.

2. *Local transit bus drivers*: Mostly 413s. Also some 411s.

3. *Local truck drivers*: Mostly in the 50s, 51s and 52–59s (esp. 531s, 541s and 521s). Also in 421s. Some Local truck drivers work for government agencies (91–97s).

4. *Long-distance truck drivers*: Mostly 421s. Also 20–39s which own

and operate their own trucks for delivery (esp. 25s and 24s). Some Long-distance truck drivers work for 01s and 02s. Many Drivers are owner-operators.

5. *Parking attendants*: 752s and some 729s (valet parking). Sometimes a business will own its own lot (70s, 58s and other 52–59s). Also some 919s.

6. *Taxicab drivers*: 412s.

7. *Shuttle bus operators*: 411s.

8. *Trolley, subway and streetcar ops.*: 411s.

8. Scientific and Technical Occupations

A. Conservation Occupations

1. *Foresters*: 26s, 24s, 951s, 08s, 822s and with Forestry management services in the 874s.

2. *Forestry technicians* (incl. Fallers and Buckers, Log graders and Scalers, Log-handling equipment operators and Logging tractor operators): Mostly 08s (esp. 085s and 082s) and 951s. This work is often seasonal during the summer or in the spring and fall fire seasons. Also 26s and 24s. Some Forestry technicians are employed in reforestation project of companies in the 10–14s and 40s.

3. *Range managers* (incl. Range scientists, Range ecologists and Range conservationists): Mostly 951s and some 964s. Also 12s, 13s, 60s and 65s (esp. 651s). Some Range managers are found in 874s and large ranches in the 01s and 02s. Range managers also work for 822s and 873s. A few Range managers work for 972s.

4. *Soil conservationists*: Mostly 951s. Also 822s as well as some 60s, 633s, 613s, 49s, 26s, 24s and 081s.

B. Engineers

1. *Aerospace*: Mostly 372s. Also some 381s, 966s and 971s. A few Aerospace engineers work for 451s, 452s, for some 871s and 822s.

2. *Agricultural*: Mostly 352s, 491s, 508s and 519s. Also some 873s, 964s, 861s and 869s. A few 20s employ Agricultural engineers as well as some 01s, 02s and 07s. Some teach on the faculties of colleges and universities (822s).

3. *Biomedical*: 871s, 822s, some 28s (esp. 283s), 873s and 966s. A few are employed by 38s (esp. 384s), 36s (esp. 369s), 357s and 508s. 806s also employ some biomedical engineers.

4. *Ceramic*: Mostly 32s. Also 33s, 36s, 372s and 28s. Some work for the 822s, 871s and 873s. A few work for the Federal Government (94–97s).

5. *Chemical* (incl. Quality control chemists): Mostly 28s and 29s.

61

Some work in government agencies (94-97s) and others do research in the 873s. A few teach in the 822s or work as consultants in the 871s.

6. *Civil*: Mostly 15-17s and for government agencies in the 94-97s. Civil engineers also work for 871s, 49s, 40s, 822s and some companies in the 20-39s.

7. *Electrical* (or electronic): Mostly 36s, 372s, 357s and 38s. Some work for 481s, 482s and 489s as well as the 491s and 493s. Many work for government agencies in the 94-97s and for colleges and universities in the 822s. A few work for the 15-17s and 871s.

8. *Industrial*: Most work for the 20-39s. Some work for 15-17s, 10-14s, 60s, 63s and 49s. Industrial engineers are also employed by 806s and large businesses in the 52-59s and other large firms. A few work for government agencies in the 94-97s and for 822s. Others work for consulting engineering firms in the 871s.

9. *Mechanical*: Mostly in the 33s, 34s, 35s and 37s. Some work in 94-97s, 822s and 824s. Mechanical engineers also work for consulting engineering firms in the 871s.

10. *Metallurgical* (incl. Extractive, Physical and Mechanical metallurgists: Also incls. Materials scientists): Mostly 33s. Some also work in the 34s, 35s, 36s, 372s and 10-14s (esp. 10s). A few work for 94-97s and 822s.

11. *Mining*: Mostly 10-14s. Some also work in the 35s, 34s, 36s and 374s. Others are employed in the 822s, 94-97s and 871s.

12. *Petroleum*: Mostly in the 13s, 29s and 35s (esp. 353s). Some also work in the 60-62s, 871s or 94-97s.

13. *Traffic*: 9621s and 871s.

C. Environmental Scientists

1. *Geologists* (incl. Economic, Petroleum, Engineering, Mineralogists, Geochemists, Volcanologists, Geomorphologists, Paleontologists, Geochronologists, Stratigraphers, Astrogeologists and Geological oceanographers): Mostly in the 13s (esp. 138s). Geologists also work for other 10-14s as well as the 15-17s and 94-97s (esp. the U.S. Geological Survey). Some Geologists are independent consultants with an 874 SIC Code and others teach in the 822s. A few Geologists work for research organizations in the 873s and 841s.

2. *Geophysicists* (incl. Solid earth, Exploration, Seismologists, Geodesists, Hydrologists, Geomagneticians, Paleomagneticians, Planetologists and Meteorologists): Most work for companies in the 13s (esp. 131s, 132s and 138s), but also in the 10-14s. Others are in the 873s and 874s as well as the 94-97s (esp. the U.S. Geological Survey, the National Oceanic and Atmospheric Administration [NOAA] and

the Defense Department). A few geophysicists teach in the 822s.

3. *Meteorologists* (incl. Synoptic, Physical and Climatologists): Mostly in the 94–97s (esp. the NOAA and the Defense Department), the 45s and the 874s. Some also work for the 38s (esp. 381s and 383s), the 372s, 63s, 871s, 49s and 483s. A few Meteorologists teach in the 822s and do research for 822s or 873s.

4. *Oceanographers* (incl. Biological, Physical, Geological, Chemical, Oceanographic engineers and Limnologists): Many work for the 822s and 94–97s (esp. the Navy and the NOAA). Some also work for the 892s and possibly for 092s.

D. Life Science Occupations

1. *Biochemists*: Most work for 822s and 28s (esp. 283s, 287s and 284s). Some work for the 892s, 873s and the 94–97s.

2. *Life scientists* (incl. Biologists, Botanists, Agronomists, Horticulturists, Zoologists, Animal scientists, Veterinarians, Anatomists, Ecologists, Embryologists, Microbiologists, Medical microbiologists, Physiologists, Pharmacologists, Toxicologists, Pathologists and Biological oceanographers): Many work in the 807s. They also teach in the 822s (esp. agricultural colleges and medical schools) and work for the 806s as well as for the Federal Government in the 94–97s (esp. 964s). Some Life scientists are employed by manufacturing firms in the 28s (esp. 283s, 286s and 287s) and the 20s. A few Life scientists work for zoological gardens in the 799s and 842s.

3. *Soil scientists*: Nearly half work for the Soil Conservation Service of the U.S. Department of Agriculture (and state agriculture departments) in the 951s. Many Soil scientists work for other state and Federal Government agencies (esp. in the 964s) and colleges of agriculture (822s). Some are employed by the 871s, 287s, 873s, 63s, 60s, 61s and 65s (esp. 653s). They are also employed by the 07s (esp. 071s, 072s, and 076s).

E. Mathematics Occupations

1. *Mathematicians*: Most are teachers in the 822s and 821s. Mathematicians also work in the 873s. Some are employed by 372s, 48s, 35s and 36s. In the Federal Government they are mostly employed by 966s and the 971s.

2. *Statisticians*: Most work in the 20–39s, 60–64s and 67s. Some work for the Federal Government in the 92–97s (esp. 96s, 93s, 94s and 97s). Others work in state and local governments and as teachers in the 822s. Some are also employed in the 874s, 873s, 737s, and 872s.

F. Physical Scientists

1. *Astronomers* (or "astrophysicists"): Most work in the 822s. In the Federal Government most astronomers are employed in 966s. Others work in the 971s and in planetariums in the 841s and 799s.

2. *Chemists*: Most chemists work for firms in the 20–39s (most of these in the 28s). Some are employed in the 822s and others work for state and local governments in the 943s and 964s. Chemists that work for the Federal Government are in the 971s and 94–96s. They also work for the 7391s and some 873s.

3. *Physicists*: Many work in the 20–39s (esp. 28s, 36s, 37s and 34s). Some work for the 806s and 873s. Other physicists teach in the 822s or work for the Federal Government in the 971s and 96s.

G. Other Scientific and Technical Occupations

1. *Broadcast technicians* (incl. Transmitter, Maintenance, Audio control, Video control, Lighting, Field, Recording and Video recording technicians, Chief engineer and Transmission engineers): Mostly 489s and 483s.

2. *Drafters* (incl. Senior drafters, Detailers, some Checkers and Tracers): Mostly 871s. Some also work for 34s, 36s, 35s and 15–17s. The Federal Government as well as state and local governments employ Drafters (mainly in the 95–97s (esp. 971s). Also, Drafters work for 822s and 873s.

3. *Engineering and science technicians* (incl. Aeronautical technicians, Air-conditioning, Heating and refrigeration, Civil engineering, Electronics, Industrial production, Mechanical, Instrumentation, Chemical, Meteorological, Geological, Hydrologic, Agricultural, Biological and Cartographic technicians): Mostly in the 36s, 28s, 35s and 372s. Many also work in the 50–59s, 48s and 871s. Some work for the Federal Government in the Defense Department (971s) and several departments in the 95s and 96s (Transportation, Agriculture, Interior and Commerce). State and local governments also employ engineering and science technicians in various departments. They also work for 822s and 873s (and some 738s).

4. *Food technologists*: Mostly in the 20s. Some do work for government agencies (mostly in the 96s and 97s). Others work for international organizations (972s) or private research and development consulting firms (873s). Food technologists are also found in the 822s and 892s.

5. *Surveyors and surveying technicians* (incl. Land surveyors, Instrument assistants, Survey helpers, Geodetic surveyors, Geophysical prospecting surveyors and Marine surveyors): Many Surveyors work for companies in the 15–17s, 871s and 4469s. Some are employed by 131s,

138s and 49s. The Federal Government hires many surveyors in the 95s, 96s and 97s. Also state and local government agencies employ Surveying technicians in in the 95s and 96s. Some mapping firms or organizations use Surveyors (other 87s and possibly some 738s).

9. Mechanics and Repairers

A. Telephone Craft Occupations

1. *Central office craft occupations* (incl. Frame wirers, Central office repairers and Trouble locators): Mostly 481s.

2. *Central offiice equipment installers*: Mostly 366s. Others work for 481s and 173s.

3. *Line installers and cable splicers*: Mostly 481s.

4. *Telephone and PBX installers and repairers*: Mostly 481s.

B. Other Mechanics and Repairers

1. *Air-conditioning, refrigeration and heating mechanics* (incl. AC&R mechanics, Furnace installers, Oil burner mechanics and Gas burner mechanics): Mostly in the 171s, 173s, 598s, 517s, 492s and 493s. Also for 541s, 82s, 20–39s and government agencies in the 91–97s.

2. *Appliance repairers*: 572s, 762s, 735s, 363s, 531s, 506s, 507s, and 492s and 493s.

3. *Automobile body repairers*: 753s, 551s, 552s, 501s. Some also work for the 41s and 42s. A few are employed by the 371 industry.

4. *Automobile mechanics* (incl. Automatic transmission specialists, Tune-up mechanics, Automobile air-conditioning specialists, Front-end mechanics, Brake mechanics, Automobile radiator mechanics and Auto glass mechanics): 551s, 552s and 501s. Also 753s, 554s and 531s with auto service facilities. Some work for government agencies (91–97s), 411s and 412s. A few also work for the 371 industry.

5. *Boat-engine mechanics*: 555s, 446s, 508s, 504s and 373s. Some work for boat rental firms in the 799s.

6. *Bowling-pin-machine mechanics*: Mostly 799s. Possibly some 179s and 394s.

7. *Business machine repairers*: Mostly for 357s. Some work for 762s, 769s. Others are employed by some of the 737s and 738s. Business machine repairers also work for companies (of most all SIC Codes) that are large enough to employ their own staff of full-time repairers.

8. *Computer service technicians*: 737s, 357s and some organizations with large computer installations.

9. *Electric sign repairers*: Mostly for 399s. Some also work for 762s.

10. *Farm equipment mechanics*: 769s, 508s and some farms in the 01s and 02s.

11. *Furniture upholsterers* (incl. Automotive upholstery repairers): Mostly for 764s. Some work for 571s and a few are employed by 701s that maintain their own furniture. Automotive upholstery repairers work for the 753s.

12. *Industrial machinery repairers* (also called Maintenance mechanics and incl. some Millwrights): Many work for the 20s, 33s, 35s, 28s, 34s, 37s, 26s and 30s. They also work for other industries that use a lot of machinery.

13. *Jewelers*: Most work for the 594s and 763s.

14. *Locksmiths*: Most work for the 769s. Some work for 525s and 531s that offer locksmith services. Some also work for government agencies in the 91–97s, for schools in the 821s and 822s and large industrial plants in the 20–39s. A few are employed by the 342s and 349s.

15. *Maintenance electricians*: Many work in the 371s, 35s, 28s and 33s. Some work for 49s, 10–14s, 40s and government agencies in the 91–97s.

16. *Motorcycle mechanics*: Most work for 557s. Others work on police motorcycles in the 922s. Some also work in the 769s.

17. *Piano and organ tuners and repairers* (incl. Piano technicians, Pipe organ repairers and Electronic organ technicians): Mostly 769s and 573s. Some are also employed by piano and organ manufacturers in the 302s.

18. *Shoe repairers*: Mostly in the 725s. Some worked in the 566s, 531s and 721s. A few were employed by shoe manufacturers in the 302s and 314s.

19. *Television and radio service technicians*: Mostly for the 762s and the 573s.

20. *Truck mechanics and bus mechanics*: Many work for the 421s, 514s and 596s. Some are employed by dealers in the 501s and manufacturers in the 371s. These kinds of mechanics also work for firms in the 753s, 421s and 751s and some work for government agencies in the 91–97s. Most Bus mechanics work for the 411s, 413s, 414s and 415s. A few work for the 371s.

21. *Vending machine mechanics*: Most work in the 596s or for companies in the 208s. Some also are employed by manufacturers in the 358s.

22. *Watch and clock repairers*: Mostly in the 594s and 763s. A few work for the 387s.

23. *Electric meter installers and repairers*: 491s and 493s.

24. *Electric motor and transformer repairers*: 769s and possibly 762s.

25. *Biomedical equipment repairers*: Possibly 807s and 769s.

26. *Electromedical equipment repairers*: Possibly 369s.

27. *Machinery maintenance workers*: 769s and 351–359s.

28. *Mobile home repairers*: 527s, 556s and possibly 753s.
29. *Rail car repairers*: 40s.
30. *Riggers*: 138s.
31. *Small engine specialists*: 769s.
32. *Tire repairers and changers*: 753s, 553s and 554s.

10. Health Occupations

A. Dental Occupations

1. *Dentists*: Mostly 802s. A few work in the armed forces (971s), Veterans Administration hospitals and Public Health Service (806s) and outpatient care facilities in the 808s.

2. *Dental assistants*: Mostly 802s. Some work in the 822s, 806s, 943s, 971s and 808s.

3. *Dental hygienists*: Mostly 802s. Some work for the 806s, 821s, industrial plants in the 20–39s, 808s, 822s and 824s. A few work for government agencies in the 943s and 971s.

4. *Dental laboratory technician*: Mostly in 807s. Some do work in the 802s, 806s, 943s and 971s. A few work for manufacturers in the 384s.

B. Medical Practitioners

1. *Chiropractors*: Mostly 804s. Possibly in chiropractic schools in the 822s or 824s.

2. *Optometrists*: Mostly 804s. Some work in the 806s and possibly in outpatient care facilities in the 808s. A few teach in schools in the 822s (or 824s).

3. *Osteopathic physicians*: Mostly 803s. Some work in the 806s and a few teach in the 822s (or 824s).

4. *Physicians* (also known as Doctors): Mostly 801s and 806s. Some work for the 873s or teach in the 822s. Physicians are also found in the armed forces (971s) and in some international development programs (972s).

5. *Podiatrists*: 804s, 806s and 822s. Some podiatrists work for public health agencies (943s) and others are officers in the armed forces (971s).

6. *Veterinarians*: Mostly in the 074s. Some work for the Federal Government in the 964s, 971s and 943s. A few work for international health agencies (972s), veterinarian or medical schools (822s), research and development labs (873s), livestock farms (029s), animal food manufacturers (204s) and pharmaceutical manufacturers (283s).

C. Medical Technologists, Technician and Assistant Occupations

1. *Electrocardiograph technicians*: Most work in cardiology depart-

ments of large hospitals (806s). Some work in smaller general hospitals or in specialty hospitals (also 806s). Other EKG technicians are employed in the 801s.

2. *Electroencephalographic technologists and technicians*: Mostly in neurology departments of hospitals (806s). Some EEG techs also work in private offices of neurologists and neurosurgeons (801s).

3. *Emergency medical technicians* (incl. ambulance attendants, EMT paramedics and EMT dispatchers): Many work for 922s and 411s. A few work for 726s and 806s.

4. *Medical laboratory workers* (incl. Medical technologists, Medical laboratory technicians and Medical laboratory assistants): Mostly in 806s. Others work in 807s, 801s, 943s, 283s and 873s. Some are also employed by the armed forces (971s).

5. *Medical record technicians and clerks*: Mostly in 806s. Some are employed by 801s, 805s, 808s, 943s, 874s and 632s (or 641s).

6. *Operating room technicians*: Mostly in 806s. Many are members of the armed forces (971s).

7. *Optometric assistants*: Mostly in 804s. Some work for clinics in the 801s and 808s. A few are in the armed forces (971).

8. *Radiologic (X-ray) technicians*: Mostly in 806s, 807s, 801s and 802s. A few work for 808s, 943s and some 821s and 822s.

9. *Respiratory therapy workers* (incl. Inhalation therapy workers): Mostly in 806s. Some work for 809s, 411s, 805s, 822s.

D. Nursing Occupations

1. *Registered nurses* (incl. Hospital nurses, Private duty nurses, Community health nurses, Office nurses, Occupational health nurses, Industrial nurses and Nurse educators): Many work for 806s and 805s. RNs also work for 808s, 943s, 82s and 862s. Some are employed in the 824s, 832s, 20–39s, 801–804s, 892s and 965s.

2. *Licensed practical nurses* (incl. Licensed vocational nurses): Mostly 806s. Some are employed by 805s and 801–804s. LPNs and LVNs also work for 808s, 866s, 943s, 832s and possibly some 836s and 839s.

3. *Nursing aides, orderlies and attendants* (incl. Hospital attendants, Nursing assistants, Auxiliary nursing workers, Geriatric aides, Psychiatric aides and Homemaker-home health aides): Mostly in 806s. Some work for 805s and possibly some 804s.

E. Therapy and Rehabilitation Occupations

1. *Occupational Therapists*: Many work in the 806s, 808s, 833s and 836s. Occupational therapists also work in the 82s, 943s, 873s and possibly 832s. Some are in the armed forces (971s).

2. *Occupational therapy assistants and aides*: Same as Occupational therapist with the addition of 835s and 821s.

3. *Physical therapists*: Mostly in 806s. Some also work in 805s and 804s. Physical therapists also are employed by 808s, 836s, 821s, 943s, 801s, 803s and other 82s. A few work for 892s, 874s and 971s.

4. *Physical therapy assistants and aides*: Mostly 806s. Also 805s, 804s, 808s, 836s, 821s, 943s, 801s, 803s and 971s.

5. *Speech pathologists and audiologists*: 821s, 822s, 873s, 806s and 808s. Private businesses (and government agencies) of various types also employ some speech pathologists and audiologists.

F. Other Health Occupations

1. *Dieticians* (incl. Administrative dieticians, Clinical dieticians, Research dieticians, Dietetic educators and Nutritionists): Many work in 806s, 805s, 804s, 808s and 943s. Dieticians also work in the 821s and 822s as well as for some 83s, 581s and 971s. Dieticians also are employed by large companies that provide food service for their employees.

2. *Dispensing opticians* (incl. Ophthalmic dispensers): 599s, 531s, 801s, 804s and 806s.

3. *Health services administrators*: 806s and 805s. Others work for 808s, 943s and 971s. A few are employed by the 873s and 839s.

4. *Medical record administrators*: Mostly in 806s. Others work in 808s, 801s, 805s, 943s, and 873s. Medical record administrators also work in 632s and 641s. A few work for printers of health insurance and medical forms (275s and 276s) and as consultants to small health care facilities (874s).

5. *Pharmacists*: 591s, 806s, 283s and 512s. This heading also includes druggists. Some work for government agencies* (91–97s) and educational institutions (82s). A few are part-time consultants (874s) to nursing homes and other health facilities. *(The Federal Government agencies are primarily: Veterans Administration, U.S. Public Health Service, Defense Department, Food and Drug Administration, HEW and the Drug Enforcement Administration). Some Pharmacists work for professional associations in the 862s.

11. Social Scientists

A. Specific Social Sciences

1. *Anthropologists* (incl. Ethnologists, Archeologists, Linguistic anthropologists, Physical anthropologists, Anthropometrists, Applied

anthropologists, Medical anthropologists and Urban anthropologists): Mostly in the 822s, 873s, government agencies (91–97s), 841s, 874s and 972s.

2. *Economists*: 20–39s, 60s, 63s, 62s, 873s, 874s, 822s and government agencies in the 91–97s.

3. *Geographers* (incl. Economic geographers, Political geographers, Physical geographers, Regional geographers, Cartographers and Medical geographers): Mostly 822s, 91–97s (esp. these Federal Government agencies: Defense Department, Interior, Commerce, Agriculture, State Department, Transportation, HEW, Energy, EPA, NASA and CIA). Some Geographers work as 873s, 874s, 953s (state and local governments), 274s, 273s, 472s, 20–39s, 655s, 63s, 48s and 47s.

4. *Historians* (incl. Archivists, Curators, Biographers and Genealogists): Mostly 822s, 823s, 841s, 873s, 862s and possibly 869s. Historians also work for the 27s and the Federal Government (primarily in the National Archives, Smithsonian Institute, General Services Administration, Defense, Interior and State Departments). Also: NASA, CIA, National Security Agency, Agriculture, Commerce, Education, Energy and Transportation. State and local governments also employ historians. Government agencies are mostly 91–97s.

5. *Political scientists*: Most work in the 822s. Others work for government agencies (91–97s), 865s, 873s and 874s. Political scientists also work for newspapers or magazines (271s, 272s, 735s or 899s), 863s, 731s and 61–62s.

6. *Psychologists* (incl. Experimental, Developmental, Personality, Social, Evaluation research, Environmental, Population, Comparative, Physiological, Psychometrics, Clinical, Counseling, Educational, School, Industrial, Organizational, Engineering, Community and Consumer psychologists): Mostly in 822s as Counselors, Researchers, Administrators or Teachers. Psychologists also work in the 806s, 8081s, 836s, 801s, 804s and 805s. They also are employed by 873s and 874s. The Federal Government agencies that hire the most psychologists are: the Veterans Administration, Defense Department and Public Health Service (806s, 945s, 971s and 943s). Other government agencies and private businesses of varied SIC Codes employ Psychologists.

7. *Sociologists*: Mostly 822s. Also 83s, 94s and 95s (esp. 944s, 945s, 951s, 953s and 971s). The Federal agencies are mainly: Defense, Health and Human Services, Education, Interior and Agriculture. Also Departments of Transportation and Energy, the Environmental Protection Agency, and the Veterans Administration. Sociologists also work in 873s, 86s and 874s.

12. Social Service Occupations

A. Counseling Occupations

1. *School counselors*: 821s.

2. *Employment counselors* (incl. Vocational counselors): Mostly for public and private services (736s and 833s). Some work in 922s and 806s. Others teach in 822s or conduct research in the 873s.

3. *Rehabilitation counselors*: Mostly 833s and other 83s. Also 806s, 863s and some 82s.

4. *College career planning and placement counselors*: 822s.

B. Clergy

1. *Protestant ministers*: Mostly for the Baptist, United Methodist, Lutheran, Presbyterian and Episcopal denominations in the 866s. Others are Chaplains in 806s, 971s or Educators in the 821s or 822s. Some Protestant ministers are employed by correctional institutions (922s).

2. *Rabbis*: Mostly orthodox, conservative or reform congregations in the 866s. Some are Chaplains in the 971s, 806s, or 922s. Others work for Jewish community service agencies (832s) or in colleges and universities (822s).

3. *Roman Catholic priests* (incl. secular [diocesan] and religious): Mostly 866s. Some Catholic priests are Chaplains, Counselors or Administrators for various institutions or agencies (however, they don't work for these agencies or institutions – they are answerable to either a diocesan bishop or a specific religious order).

C. Other Social Service Occupations (incl. Welfare workers)

1. *Cooperative Extension Service workers* (incl. Extension agents or Agricultural Extension agents): Mostly for county government agencies in the 964s. Some do work for state agencies (same SIC Code) and a few work for the Federal Agricultural Extension Service of the U.S. Department of Agriculture (also 964).

2. *Homemaker-Home health aides*: Most are employed by public health and/or welfare agencies (943s) and (832s). They also work for 809s and possibly some 839s. A few Homemaker–Home health aides are employed by 806s and 805s.

3. *Social Service aides* (incl. Income maintenance workers, Casework aides or assistants, Neighborhood workers, Outreach workers and Employment aides): Most work for 83s (esp. 832s) and 866s. Some work for 806s, 821s and 822s. A few work for public housing projects (651s).

4. *Social workers*: Mostly for the 83s and 86s. Some work in 806s, 821s and 822s. Social workers are employed by all levels of government as well as private organizations. They work as Planners and Administrators for government agencies in the 94s and 95s. A few work for 972s and 874s. A small number of social workers are also employed in business and industry (various SIC Codes).

5. *Eligibility workers (incl. Interviewers): 83s, 944s and 953s.*

13. Performing Arts, Design, and Communications

A. Performing Artists

1. *Actors and actresses*: 792s and 781s.

2. *Dancers* (incl. Dance therapy): 792s and 781s. Dancers also teach in 791, 821s and 822s. Dance therapists work for 806s, 943s, 922s and 821s.

3. *Musicians* (incl. "popular," "classical," "folk" and "jazz"): Mostly 792s and 365s. Some teach in 821s, 822s and 829s. Musicians are also employed by 899s, 738s, 769s, 593s, 573s, 509s and 519s. Musicians sometimes work as Therapists in 806s and 943s. Some popular and jazz Musicians are employed by night clubs (581s). Church Musicians work for the 866s. A few Musicians make a career of the armed forces (directing a military band) in the 971s.

4. *Singers* (incl. Vocalists or Vocal musicians): Many work for 792s and 365s. Others teach in 821s, 822s and 829s. Many Singers are employed by churches and synagogues and some by singing societies in the 864s. Singers are also found in the armed forces (971s).

B. Design Occupations

1. *Architects*: Mostly 871s, 15s and 65s. Some Architects work for state and local governments in the 953s. Architects also work for the Federal Government in the 971s, Interior Department (951s), Housing and Urban Development (953s) and General Services Administration (919s). Architects are also employed by a variety of private businesses that have large construction programs.

2. *Artists* (incl. Commerical, Non-commercial, Graphic artists and Graphic designers): 733s, 824s, 829s and some 87s.

3. *Display workers* (incl. Merchandise displayers, Model dressers, Showcase trimmers, Window dressers and Commercial decorators): Mostly in the 531s, 56s, 571s and 572s. Display workers are also employed by 533s, 591s, 566s and 594s. Some also work for 738s, 731s and 874s.

4. *Floral designers* (incl. Florists): 599s.

5. *Industrial designers*: Most work for large manufacturing companies (20–39s) or for design consulting firms (874s and/or 738s). Others work for 871s or teach in the 822s and 824s.

6. *Interior designers* (incl. Interior decorators): Mostly 824s and 738s. Some work for large 531s or 571s. Others are employed by large hotels (701s) and restaurant chains (581s), by builders (15s), government agencies (953s) and other organizations that do a lot of building. Interior designers also work for 871s, 502s, 593s and manufacturers in the 25s, 22s and some 272s.

7. *Landscape architects*: Mostly 078s and 871s. Some work for government agencies: forest management (085s), water storage (49s), public housing and urban renewal (953s), city planning (874s), highways (962s and 16s), parks and recreation departments (951s and 799s). The Federal Government hires Landscape architects in the Defense Department (971s), Agriculture Department (96s) and Interior Department (95s). Landscape architects also teach in the 822s.

8. *Photographers* (incl. Portrait photographers, Commercial photographers, Industrial photographers and Photojournalists and Freelance photographers): Mostly 733s. Many others work for the 271s and 272s. Photographers also work for a variety of government agencies (91–97s), 504s, 594s and industrial firms in the 20–39s. Some Photographers teach in the 822s (or 722s) or make films (781s). Others freelance and sell to advertisers and magazines.

C. Communications Occupations

1. *Newspaper reporters*: Mostly 735s and 271s.

2. *Public relations workers* (incl. Public information officers and Consumer services, Customer relations and Customer services personnel): Many work for manufacturing firms (20–39s), public utilities (49s), transportation companies (40s, 41s, 44s and 45s), insurance companies (63s and 64s) and associations in the 86s (esp. 861–863s). Some work for various government agencies (91–97s), schools (821s and 822s), museums (799s and 841s), libraries (823s) and various social service organizations (83s). Public relations workers also work for public and private health agencies (80s) and pharmaceutical companies (283s). Some Public relations workers are employed by consulting firms (874s) and advertising agencies (731s).

3. *Radio and television announcers*: Mostly 483s and some 87s. Some freelance to advertising agencies (731s).

4. *Technical writers*: Large firms in the 36s, 372s, 348s, 28s (esp. 283s) and 357s. Technical writers also work for 49s, 48s, 737s and 873s. Some Technical writers are employed by manufacturing laboratories

in the 20–39s (and also in the 873s). The 874s also hire Technical writers as well as government agencies in the 91–97s (the Federal Government hires for the Defense Department (971), Interior Department (95s), Agriculture Department (96s), Human Services and Education Departments (94s) and NASA (966s). Many Technical writers work directly for publishers in the 27s (esp. 272s, 273s and 274s). Technical writers work in 822s, 806s, 86s and 731s.

5. *Newspaper publishers* (incl. larger Newsletter publishers): 271s.

6. *Magazine publishers*: 272s.

7. *Book publishers*: 273s.

8. *Proof readers* (publishing and printing): 271s, 272s and 273s.

14. Sports, Recreation, and Amusement Occupations

A. Commercial Sports Occupations (selected)

1. *Professional sports club operators, promoters and workers* (incl. Sports arena operators and workers, Sports event promoters, Managers, Coaches, Batboys, Players (incl. baseball, basketball, ice hockey, tennis, football, golf, soccer, etc.): 794s.

2. *Race track operators and workers* (incl. horse, car, motorcycle, dragster, stock car, etc.): 794s.

B. Recreation and Amusement Occupations (selected)

1. *Amusement park operators and workers*: 799s.

2. *Amusement concessions and rides operators and workers*: 799s.

3. *Animal show operators and workers* (incl. Lion tamers): 799s.

4. *Arcade operators and workers*: 799s.

5. *Billiard and pool hall operators and workers*: 799s.

6. *Bowling alley operators and workers*: 799s.

7. *Circus operators and workers* (incl. Tight-rope walkers): 799s.

8. *Coaches* (for non-commerical or amateur sports – incl. Little League baseball. Also includes Managers): 799s, 821s and 822s.

9. *Golf course operators and workers*: 799s.

10. *Recreation services operators and workers*: 799s.

11. *Sporting goods and equipment rental operators and workers*: 799s.

12. *Sports and recreation club operators and workers: membership* (incl. Athletic clubs and gymnasiums): 799s.

13. *Sports and recreation club operators and workers: non-membership* (incl. some gymnasiums): 799s.

14. *Sports instructors and teachers* (incl. golf, swimming, tennis, etc.): 821s, 822s, and 799s.

15. *Swimming pool operators and workers* (*not* cleaners or caretakers): 799s.

16. *Tennis court operators*: 799s.

17. *Ticket takers and ticket sales office operators and workers*: 783s, 792s, 794s and 799s.

18. *Aerobic dance instructors*: 799s and possibly some 791s.

19. *Dance instructors*: 791s.

20. *Ushers* (incl. Lobby attendants): 783s, 792s, 784s and possibly some 799s.

15. Agriculture and Related Occupations

A. Farm Production Occupations

1. *Farm operators*: 01s and 02s.

2. *Farm laborers* (incl. Farm hands, Tenant farmers, Irrigators, Produce sorters, Produce packers and Farm labor supervisors): 01s and 02s.

3. *Plant farming*: 01s and 072s.

4. *Animal farming*: 02s and 075s.

B. Agricultural Services Occupations

1. *Veterinarians* (see: "Veterinarian" section under **Health Occupations**/Medical Practitioners).

*2. *Animal breeders*: 075s.

*3. *Artificial breeding technicians* (incl. Artificial inseminators and Artificial breeding distributors): 075s.

  *(2 and 3 are also employed by animal breeding associations in the 861s.)

4. *Cow testers*: 075s.

5. *Cattle dehorners*: 075s.

6. *Poultry caretakers*: 075s.

7. *Farm managers*: 0762s.

8. *Agricultural pilots* (Crop-dusters): 072s.

9. *Grain preparation services*: 072s.

10. *Farm labor contractors* (incl. Crew leaders): 076s.

11. *Animal caretakers* (nonfarm): 842s, 074s, 873s, 919s, 075s, 027s, 794s and some 799s.

C. Agribusiness Occupations (professional and technical)

1. *Agricultural accountants*: 52s, 508s, 01s, 02s and 07s.

2. *Agricultural marketing specialists*: 20s, 508s, 515s and other manufacturers (21-39s). They also work for commodity brokers (622s), farm organizations (861s) and Federal Government research divisions (873s) or (964s).

3. *Agricultural economists*: 961s, 874s, 613s, 352s, 633s, 51s and 54s. Some Agricultural economists teach in the 822s and conduct research for 972s.

4. *Agricultural communicators* (incl. Crop reporters, Market news reporters and Agricultural journalists): 961s, 272s, 483s. Agricultural communicators are also employed by communication departments of large agribusiness firms or organizations (incl. manufacturers, trade associations and agricultural service companies). They can also work for public relations firms (874s) or advertising agencies (731s).

5. *Agricultural school teachers*: 82s.

6. *Cooperative Extension Service workers* (*see* section under "Social Service Occupations/Other Social Service Occupations.")

7. *Life scientists (see* "Life Science Occupations/Life Scientists.")

8. *Agricultural commodity graders*: 964s and buyers of large quantities of agricultural commodities.

9. *Farm equipment sales worker*: 508s, 519s and some 52s. Some work for manufacturers of farm machinery and equipment (352s).

D. Fish Farming: 027s.

E. Fishery Workers: 091s.

F. Fish Hatchery Workers: 092s.

G. Hunting: 097s.

H. Trapping: 097s.

16. Mining and Petroleum Occupations

A. Mining Occupations
   1. *Mining operatives*: 10s, 11s, 12s and 14s.
   2. *Mining inspectors*: 10s, 11s, 12s and 14s.
   3. *Mining shift boss*: 10s, 11s, 12s and 14s.
   4. *Preparation plant operators*: 10s, 11s, 12s and 14s.
   5. *Preparation plant supervisors*: 10s, 11s, 12s, and 14s.
   6. *Mining administrators*: 10s, 11s, 12s and 14s.
   7. *Mining professionals* (Engineers, etc.): 10s, 11s, 12s and 14s.
   8. *Mining clerical workers*: 10s, 11s, 12s and 14s.
   9. *Mining technical personnel* (Surveyors, etc.): 10s, 11s, 12s and 14s.

B. Occupations in Petroleum and Natural Gas

1. *Oil and gas exploration crews*: 13s (esp. 138s).
2. *Oil and gas drilling personnel*: 13s (esp. 138s).
3. *Oil well operators*: 13s (also 871s).
4. *Oil well maintenance personnel*: 13s (esp. 138s).
5. *Natural gas processing personnel*: 13s (esp. 131s and 132s).
6. *Oilfield services personnel*: 13s (esp. 138s).
7. *Offshore oil exploration*: 13s.
8. *Roustabouts*: 13s (esp. 138s, 131s, and 132s).
 9. *Oil and gas derrick operators*: 13s.

C. Occupations in Petroleum Refining: 291s.

SIC Code List

exc.   *except*
misc.   *miscellaneous*
nec.   *not elsewhere classified*

—a. (Agriculture, Forestry and Fishing)

01 Agricultural Production — Crops
011 Cash Grains
013 Field Crops, Exc. Cash Grains
016 Vegetables and Melons
017 Fruits and Tree Nuts
018 Horticultural Specialties
019 General Farms, Primarily Crop

02 Agricultural Production — Livestock
021 Livestock, exc. Dairy, Poultry, etc.
024 Dairy Farms
025 Poultry and Eggs
027 Animal Specialties
029 Genl. Farms, Primarily Livestock

07 Agricultural Services
071 Soil Preparation Services
072 Crop Services
074 Veterinary Services
075 Animal Services, Exc. Vets.
076 Farm Labor and Mangmt. Svcs.

078 Landscape and Horticultural Svcs.

08 Forestry
081 Timber Tracts
083 Forest Products, Exc. Timber
085 Forestry Services

09 Fishing, Hunting and Trapping
091 Commercial Fishing
092 Fish Hatcheries and Preserves
097 Hunting, Trapping and Game Propagation

—b. (Mining)

10 Metal Mining
101 Iron Ores
102 Copper Ores
103 Lead and Zinc Ores
104 Gold and Silver Ores
106 Ferroalloy Ores, Exc. Vanadium
108 Metal Mining Services
109 Miscellaneous Metal Ores

12 Bituminous Coal and Lignite Mining
122 Bituminous Coal and Lignite

123 Anthracite Mining
124 Coal Mining Services

13 Oil and Gas Extraction
131 Crude Petroleum and Natural Gas
132 Natural Gas Liquids
138 Oil and Gas Field Svcs.

14 Nonmetallic Minerals, Exc. Fuels
141 Dimension Stone
142 Crushed and Broken Stone
144 Sand and Gravel
145 Clay and Related Materials
147 Chemical and Fertilizer Minerals
148 Nonmetallic Minerals Svcs.
149 Misc. Nonmetallic Minerals

—c. (Construction)

15 General Building Contractors
152 Residential Building Construction
153 Operative Builders
154 Nonresidential Building Construction

16 Heavy Construction Contractors
161 Highways and Street Construction
162 Heavy Construction, Exc. Highways

17 Special Trade Contractors
171 Plumbing, Heating and Air Conditioning
172 Painting, Paper Hanging, Decorating

173 Electrical Work
174 Masonry, Stonework and Plastering
175 Carpentering and Flooring
176 Roofing and Sheet Metal Work
177 Concrete Work
178 Water Well Drilling
179 Miscellaneous Special Trade Contractors

—d. (Manufacturing)

20 Food and Kindred Products
201 Meat Products
202 Dairy Products
203 Preserved Fruits and Vegetables
204 Grain Mill Products
205 Bakery Products
206 Sugar and Confectionery Products
207 Fats and Oils
208 Beverages
209 Miscellaneous Foods and Kindred Products

21 Tobacco Manufacturers
211 Cigarettes
212 Cigars
213 Chewing and Smoking Tobacco
214 Tobacco Stemming and Redrying

22 Textile Mill Products
221 Broadwoven Fabric Mills, Cotton
222 Broadwoven Fabric Mills, Manmade
223 Broadwoven Fabric Mills, Wool

224 Narrow Fabric Mills
225 Knitting Mills
226 Textile Finishing, Exc. Wool
227 Carpets and Rugs
228 Yarn and Thread Mills
229 Miscellaneous Textile Goods

23 Apparel and Other Textile Products

231 Men's and Boys' Suits and Coats
232 Men's and Boys' Furnishings
233 Women's and Misses' Outerwear
234 Women's and Children's Undergarments
235 Hats, Caps and Millinery
236 Girls' and Children's Outerwear
237 Fur Goods
238 Misc. Apparel and Accessories
239 Misc. Fabricated Textile Products

24 Lumber and Wood Products

241 Logging
242 Sawmills and Planing Mills
243 Millwork, Plywood and Structural Members
244 Wood Containers
245 Wood Buildings and Mobile Homes
249 Misc. Wood Products

25 Furniture and Fixtures

251 Household Furniture
252 Office Furniture
253 Public Building and Related Furniture
254 Partitions and Fixtures
259 Misc. Furniture and Fixtures

26 Paper and Allied Products

261 Pulp Mills
262 Paper Mills, Exc. Building Paper
263 Paperboard Mills
265 Paperboard Containers and Boxes
267 Misc. Converted Paper Products

27 Printing and Publishing

271 Newspapers
272 Periodicals
273 Books
274 Miscellaneous Publishing
275 Commercial Printing
276 Manifold Business Forms
277 Greeting Cards
278 Blankbooks and Bookbinding
279 Printing Trade Services

28 Chemicals and Allied Products

281 Industrial Inorganic Chemicals
282 Plastics Materials and Synthetics
283 Drugs
284 Soap, Cleaners and Toilet Goods
285 Paints and Allied Products
286 Industrial Organic Chemicals
287 Agricultural Chemicals
289 Misc. Chemical Products

29 Petroleum and Coal Products

291 Petroleum Refining
295 Asphalt Paving and Roofing Materials
299 Misc. Petroleum and Coal Products

30 Rubber and Misc. Plastic Products

301 Tires and Inner Tubes
302 Rubber and Plastics Footwear
305 Hose and Belting and Gaskets and Packing
306 Fabricated Rubber Products, NEC.
308 Misc. Plastics Products, NEC.

31 Leather and Leather Products

311 Leather Tanning and Finishing
313 Footware Cut Stock
314 Footwear, Exc. Rubber
315 Leather Gloves and Mittens
316 Luggage
317 Handbags and Personal Leather Goods
319 Leather Goods, NEC.

32 Stone, Clay and Glass Products

321 Flat Glass
322 Glass and Glassware, Pressed or Blown
323 Products of Purchased Glass
324 Cement, Hydraulic
325 Structural Clay Products
326 Pottery and Related Products
327 Concrete, Gypsum and Plaster Products
328 Cut Stone and Stone Products
329 Misc. Nonmetalic Mineral Products

33 Primary Metal Industries

331 Blast Furnace and Basic Steel Products
332 Iron and Steel Foundries
333 Primary Nonferrous Metals
334 Secondary Nonferrous Metals
335 Nonferrous Rolling and Drawing
336 Nonferrous Foundries (Castings)
339 Misc. Primary Metal Products

34 Fabricated Metal Products

341 Metal Cans and Shipping Containers
342 Cutlery, Hand Tools and Hardware
343 Plumbing and Heating, Exc. Electric
344 Fabricated Structural Metal Products
345 Screw Machine Products, Bolts, etc.
346 Metal Forgings and Stampings
347 Metal Services, NEC.
348 Ordinance and Accessories, NEC.
349 Misc. Fabricated Metal Products

35 Industrial Machinery and Equipment

351 Engines and Turbines
352 Farm and Garden Machinery
353 Construction and Related Machinery
354 Metalworking Machinery
355 Special Industry Machinery
356 General Industrial Machinery
357 Computer and Office Equipment

358 Refrigeration and Service Machinery

359 Industrial Machinery, NEC.

36 Electronic and Other Electric Equipment

361 Electric Distribution Equipment

362 Electrical Industrial Apparatus

363 Household Appliances

364 Electric Lighting and Wiring Equipment

365 Household AV Equipment

366 Communications Equipment

367 Electronic Components and Accessories

369 Miscellaneous Electrical Equipment and Supplies

37 Transportation Equipment

371 Motor Vehicles and Equipment

372 Aircraft and Parts

373 Ship and Boat Building and Repairing

374 Railroad Equipment

375 Motorcycles, Bicycles and Parts

376 Guided Missiles, Space Vehicles, Parts

379 Miscellaneous Transportation Equipment

38 Instruments and Related Products

381 Search and Navigation Equipment

382 Measuring and Controlling Devices

384 Medical Instruments and Supplies

385 Opthalmic Goods

386 Photographic Equipment and Supplies

387 Watches, Clocks and Watchcases and Parts

39 Misc. Manufacturing Industries

391 Jewelry, Silverware and Plated Ware

393 Musical Instruments

394 Toys and Sporting Goods

395 Pens, Pencils, Office and Art Supplies

396 Costume Jewelry and Notions

399 Misc. Manufacturers

—e. (Transportation and Public Utilities)

40 Railroad Transportation

401 Railroads

41 Local and Interurban Passenger Transit

411 Local and Suburban Transportation

412 Taxicabs

413 Intercity and Rural Bus Transportation

414 Bus Charter Svc.

415 School Buses

417 Bus Terminal and Service Facilities

42 Trucking and Warehousing

421 Trucking and Courier Services, Exc. Air

422 Public Warehousing and Storage

423 Trucking Terminal Facilities

43 U.S. Postal Service
431 U.S. Postal Service

44 Water Transportation
441 Deep Sea Foreign Trans. of Freight
442 Deep Sea Domestic Trans. of Freight
443 Freight Trans. on the Great Lakes
444 Water Trans. of Freight, NEC
448 Water Trans. of Passengers
449 Water Transportation Services

45 Transportation by Air
451 Air Transportation, Scheduled
452 Air Transportation, Non-scheduled
458 Airports, Flying Fields and Services

46 Pipe Lines, Exc. Natural Gas
461 Pipe Lines, Exc. Natural Gas

47 Transportation Services
472 Passenger Transportation Arrangement
473 Freight Transportation Arrangement
474 Rental of Railroad Cars
478 Misc. Transportation Services

48 Communication
481 Telephone Communications
482 Telegraph and Other Communications
483 Radio and TV Broadcasting
484 Cable and Other Pay TV Services
489 Communication Services, NEC.

49 Electric, Gas and Sanitary Svcs.
491 Electrical Services
492 Gas Production and Distribution
493 Combination Utility Svcs.
494 Water Supply
495 Sanitary Services
496 Steam and Air-Conditioning Supply
497 Irrigation Systems

—f. (Wholesale Trade)

50 Wholesale Trade—Durable Goods
501 Motor Vehicles, Parts and Supplies
502 Furniture and Home Furnishings
503 Lumber and Construction Materials
504 Professional and Commercial Equipment
505 Metals and Minerals, Exc. Petroleum
506 Electrical Goods
507 Hardware, Plumbing and Heating Equipment
508 Machinery, Equipment and Supplies
509 Miscellaneous Durable Goods

51 Wholesale Trade— Nondurable Goods
511 Paper and Paper Products

512 Drugs, Proprietaries and Sundries
513 Apparel, Piece Goods and Notions
514 Groceries and Related Products
515 Farm-Product Raw Materials
516 Chemicals and Allied Products
517 Petroleum and Petroleum Products
518 Beer, Wine and Distilled Beverages
519 Miscellaneous Nondurable Goods

—g. (Retail Trade)

52 Building Materials and Garden Supplies
521 Lumber and Other Building Materials
523 Paint, Glass and Wallpaper Stores
525 Hardware Stores
526 Retail Nurseries and Garden Stores
527 Mobile Home Dealers

53 General Merchandise Stores
531 Department Stores
533 Variety Stores
539 Misc. General Merchandise Stores

54 Food Stores
541 Grocery Stores
542 Meat and Fish Markets
543 Fruit and Vegetable Markets
544 Candy, Nut and Confectionery Stores
545 Dairy Products Stores
546 Retail Bakeries
549 Miscellaneous Food Stores

55 Automotive Dealers and Service Stations
551 New and Used Car Dealers
552 Used Car Dealers
553 Auto and Home Supply Stores
554 Gasoline Service Stations
555 Boat Dealers
556 Recreation Vehicle Dealers
557 Motorcycle Dealers
559 Automotive Dealers, NEC.

56 Apparel and Accessory Stores
561 Men's and Boys' Clothing Stores
562 Women's Clothing Stores
563 Women's Accessory and Specialty Stores
564 Children's and Infants' Wear Stores
565 Family Clothing Stores
566 Shoe Stores
569 Misc. Apparel and Accessory Stores

57 Furniture and Home Furnishings Stores
571 Furniture and Home Furnishings Stores
572 Household Appliance Stores
573 Radio, Television and Computer Stores

58 Eating and Drinking Places
581 Eating and Drinking Places

59 Miscellaneous Retail
591 Drug Stores and Proprietary Stores

592 Liquor Stores
593 Used Merchandise Stores
594 Miscellaneous Shopping Goods Stores
596 Nonstore Retailers
598 Fuel Dealers
599 Retail Stores, NEC.

— *h. (Finance, Insurance and Real Estate*

60 Depository Institutions
601 Central Reserve Depositories
602 Commercial Banks
603 Savings Institutions
606 Credit Unions
608 Foreign Banks and Branches and Agencies
609 Functions Closely Related to Banking

61 NonDepository Institutions
611 Federal and Fed.-Sponsored Credit
614 Personal Credit Institutions
615 Business Credit Institutions
616 Mortgage Bankers and Brokers

62 Security and Commodity Brokers
621 Security Brokers and Dealers
622 Commodity Contracts Brokers, Dealers
623 Security and Commodity Exchanges
628 Security and Commodity Services

63 Insurance Carriers
631 Life Insurance
632 Medical Service and Health Insurance

633 Fire, Marine and Casualty Insurance
635 Surety Insurance
636 Title Insurance
637 Pension, Health and Welfare Funds
639 Insurance Carriers, NEC.

64 Insurance Agents, Brokers and Service
641 Insurance Agents, Brokers and Service

65 Real Estate
651 Real Estate Operators and Lessors
653 Real Estate Agents and Managers
654 Title Abstract Offices
655 Subdividers and Developers

67 Holding and Other Investment Offices
671 Holding Offices
672 Investment Offices
673 Trusts
679 Miscellaneous Investing

— *i. (Services)*

70 Hotels and Other Lodging Places
701 Hotels and Motels
702 Rooming and Boarding Houses
703 Camps and RV Parks
704 Membership-Basis Organization Hotels

72 Personal Services
721 Laundry, Cleaning and Garment Services

722 Photographic Studios, Portrait
723 Beauty Shops
724 Barber Shops
725 Shoe Repair and Shoeshine Parlors
726 Funeral Service and Crematories
729 Misc. Personal Services

73 Business Services
731 Advertising
732 Credit Reporting and Collection
733 Mailing, Reproduction, Stenographic
734 Services to Buildings
735 Misc. Equipment, Rental and Leasing
736 Personnel Supply Services
737 Computer and Data Processing Services
738 Misc. Business Services

75 Auto Repair, Services and Parking
751 Automotive Rentals, No Drivers
752 Automobile Parking
753 Automotive Repair Shops
754 Automotive Services, Exc. Repair

76 Misc. Repair Services
762 Electrical Repair Shops
763 Watch, Clock and Jewelry Repair
764 Reupholstery and Furniture Repair
769 Misc. Repair Shops

78 Motion Pictures
781 Motion Picture Production and Services
782 Motion Picture Distribution and Services
783 Motion Picture Theaters
784 Video Tape Rental

79 Amusement and Recreation Services
791 Dance Studios, Schools and Halls
792 Producers, Orchestras, Entertainers
793 Bowling Centers
794 Commercial Sports
799 Misc. Amusement and Recreational Services

80 Health Services
801 Offices and Clinics of Medical Doctors
802 Offices and Clinics of Dentists
803 Offices of Osteopathic Physicians
804 Offices of Other Health Practitioners
805 Nursing and Personal Care Facilities
806 Hospitals
807 Medical and Dental Laboratories
808 Home Health Care Services
809 Health and Allied Services, NEC.

81 Legal Services
811 Legal Services

82 Educational Services
821 Elementary and Secondary Schools

822 Colleges and Universities
823 Libraries
824 Vocational Schools
829 Schools and Educational Services, NEC.

83 Social Services
832 Individual and Family Services
833 Job Training and Related Services
835 Child Day Care Services
836 Residential Care
839 Social Services, NEC.

84 Museums, Botanical and Zoological Gardens
841 Museums and Art Galleries
842 Botanical and Zoological Gardens

86 Membership Organizations
861 Business Associations
862 Professional Organizations
863 Labor Organizations
864 Civic and Social Associations
865 Political Organizations
866 Religious Organizations
869 Membership Organizations, NEC.

87 Engineering and Management Services
871 Engineering and Architectural Services
872 Accounting, Auditing and Bookkeeping
873 Research and Testing Services
874 Management and Public Relations (Incl. Consultants, etc.)

88 Private Households
881 Private Households

89 Services, NEC.
899 Services, NEC.

—j. (Public Administration)

91 Executive, Legislative and General
911 Executive Offices
912 Legislative Bodies
913 Executive and Legislative Combined
919 General Government, NEC.

92 Justice, Public Order and Safety
921 Courts
922 Public Order and Safety

93 Finance, Taxation and Monetary Policy
931 Finance, Taxation and Monetary Policy

94 Administration of Human Resources
941 Administration of Educational Programs
943 Administration of Public Health Programs
944 Administration of Social, Human Resource and Income Maintenance Programs
945 Administration of Veterans' Affairs

95 Environmental Quality and Housing
951 Environmental Quality
953 Housing and Urban Development

96 Administration of Economic Programs

961 Administration of General Economic Programs

962 Regulation, Administration of Transportation

963 Regulation and Administration of Communications, Electric, Gas and Other Utilities

964 Regulation of Agricultural Marketing and Commodities

965 Regulation of Misc. Commercial Sectors

966 Space Research and Technology

97 National Security and International Affairs

971 National Security

972 International Affairs

—*k. (Nonclassifiable Establishments)*

99 Nonclassifiable Establishments

999 Nonclassifiable Establishments

Bibliography

I. The Standard Industrial Classification Manual

Although the SIC manual by itself doesn't have information on jobs or job titles, it does have a large listing of types of companies and government agencies. Its index of manufacturing and nonmanufacturing industries is quite helpful in determining the SIC code number for a particular company.

Executive Office of the President, Office of Management and Budget. *Standard Industrial Classification Manual.* Springfield VA: U.S. Dept. of Commerce, National Technical Information Service, 1987.

II. Directories Using the SIC Code System

These directories classify companies by SIC codes and can therefore be used in conjunction with *Job Title Index to SIC Codes.* (See "How to Use This Book," p. 13.)

If you are looking for a job in your own geographic area, it is probably best to start with local and regional business directories, chamber of commerce directories (available from most cities or counties), and state industrial, manufacturing and service directories. Your nearest public library should have these for your use; if not, the staff can probably refer you to a larger library in your city or county that would have these directories and possibly some of the others on this list. (One source of state industrial, manufacturing or service directories is MacRae's State Industrial Directories, MacRae's Blue Book, Inc., 817 Broadway, New York NY 10003. A list of other publishers of state industrial directories is available from Manufacturer's News, Inc., 4 E. Huron St., Chicago IL 60611.)

In terms of numbers of companies listed for each SIC code, *Contacts Influential* is probably the best book for the most people, but only if they want to work in an area where there is one published (see entry, below). These books are expensive and are available on a lease basis only, so your library may not be able to afford one. Most libraries have only the edition that covers their particular area.

Nationwide directories such as *Dun and Bradstreet's Million-Dollar Dirctory* feature a listing of some of the larger publicly held stock companies. Some directories do include privately held companies, including some fairly small companies, but not many. Most nationwide directories have geographic indexes so you can choose the area(s) you want to work in. Nationwide directories are marked with [Natl] in the entries below.

Worldwide directories, such as *Principal International Businesses*, include some of the larger companies for each country. For those who want to work abroad, these are a good starting point (as is *Directory of American Firms Operating in Foreign Countries* in Part II of this Bibliography). International directories are marked with [Intl] in the entries below.

Bibliography

Contacts Influential. Published by seventeen Contacts Influential International Corporation franchises nationwide, including Tucson AZ, Foster City CA, Long Beach CA, San Francisco CA, San Jose CA, Arvada CO, Tampa FL, Atlanta GA, Chicago IL, St. Paul MN, Kansas City MO, St. Louis MO, Cleveland OH, Portland OR, Arlington TX, and Seattle WA. 1958 – (yearly).

Directory of Corporate Affiliations. Wilmette IL: National Register Publishing Corp., 1976 – (yearly). [Natl]

Dun & Bradstreet's Million-Dollar Directory. New York: Dun and Bradstreet, 1979 – (yearly). [Natl]

Dun's Business Rankings. New York: Dun & Bradstreet, 1982 – (yearly). [Natl]

Dun's Industrial Guide. Dun and Bradstreet Marketing Services, 1981 – (yearly). [Natl]

Dun's Latin America's Top 25,000. Dun & Bradstreet Marketing Services, 1984 – (yearly). [Intl]

International Directory of Corporate Affiliations. Wilmette IL: National Register Publishing Corp., 1981 – (yearly). [Intl]

National Directory of Addresses and Telephone Numbers. New York: Concord Reference Books, 1979 – (yearly). [Natl]

Principal International Business Directories. New York: Dun and Bradstreet International, 1975 – (yearly). [Intl]

Standard & Poor's Register of Corporations, Directors and Executives. New York: Standard, 1942 – (yearly). [Natl]

Standard Directory of Advertisers. Wilmette IL: National Register Publishing Corp., 1964 – (yearly). [Natl]

Ward's Business Directory. Vol. 1, *Largest U.S. Companies* [Natl]. Vol. 2, *Major U.S. Private Companies* [Natl]. Vol. 3, *Major International Companies* [Intl]. Belmont, CA: Information Access, 1985 – (yearly).

II. Other Helpful Job Reference Sources

Below are listed some general career reference books, most of which can be found in most large public libraries and some small ones. They are mainly helpful if you are not sure what kind of job you want and you need a handle on what's out there. Taken separately, each of these books has a different emphasis, but taken together they contain quite a large body of knowledge of the working world.

Bolles, Richard N. *What Color Is Your Parachute? A Practical Manual for Job-Hunters and Career-Changers.* Berkeley CA: Ten Speed, 1972 – (yearly).

Crystal, John, and _____. *Where Do I Go from Here with My Life? A Workbook for Career Seekers and Career Changers.* New York: Seabury, 1974.

Directory of American Firms Operating in Foreign Countries. New York: Uniworld Business Publications, 1907 – (at various intervals).

Encyclopedia of Careers and Vocational Guidance. New York: Doubleday, 1967 – (every three years).

Feingold and Miller. *Emerging Careers.* Garrett Park MD: Garrett Park Press, 1983.

Hawes, Gene. *Encyclopedia of Second Careers.* New York: Facts on File, 1984.

Bibliography

Leape, Martha. *Harvard Guide to Careers.* Cambridge MA: Harvard University Press, 1983.

Russo, JoAnn. *Careers Without College: No B.S. Necessary.* White Hall VA: Betterway Publications, 1985.

United States Department of Labor. *Dictionary of Occupational Titles.* 4th ed. Washington DC: U.S. Government Printing Office, 1977.

United States Department of Labor, Bureau of Labor Statistics. *Occupational Outlook Handbook.* Washington DC: U.S. Government Printing Office, 1949 — (every two years).